AMERICAN THiNK

STUDENT'S BOOK STARTER

Herbert Puchta, Jeff Stranks & Peter Lewis-Jones

CAMBRIDGE
UNIVERSITY PRESS

CONTENTS

The /ɔ/ vowel sound	**Values:** The importance of sports **Self-esteem:** My time: pie chart	**Reading** **Listening** **Writing**	Short articles: They're good! Article: The other final Photostory: The big game Phone call: Making arrangements Paragraph: My favorite sportsperson
Intonation: listing items	**Values:** Music **Train to Think:** Memorizing	**Reading** **Listening** **Writing**	Tweets: #musicinsupermarket Dialogue: A conversation at a party Culture: Musical instruments around the world Radio phone-in: Dances around the world Tweets: Describing a scene
Intonation: giving two choices	**Values:** How you eat is important **Self-esteem:** You are what you eat	**Reading** **Listening** **Writing**	Article: Young kitchen stars Menu and dialogue: In a café Photostory: The pizza Description: Describing a picture Menu: A meal plan for your friend
Simple past: regular verbs	**Values:** Hard work and achievement **Train to Think:** Sequencing	**Reading** **Listening** **Writing**	Article: It was her dream to be an astronaut Article: Fictional heroes Culture: Statues Dialogue: Ethan's Saturday evening Proposal: A statue in my town
Simple past: irregular verbs	**Values:** Animals and us **Self-esteem:** Animals and nature	**Reading** **Listening** **Writing**	Article: Erin and Tonk to the rescue Article: Extinct animals Photostory: The spider Dialogue: Bella's vacation Blog entry: A day in the life of an animal
Word stress: comparatives	**Values:** Transportation and the environment **Train to Think:** Comparing	**Reading** **Listening** **Writing**	Article: The great race Article: My favorite trip Culture: Transportation around the world Dialogue: At the train station Description: Unusual forms of transportation

7 WE LOVE SPORTS!

OBJECTIVES

FUNCTIONS: talking about abilities; telling time; talking about routines and dates; making suggestions

GRAMMAR: *can / can't* for ability; prepositions of time

VOCABULARY: sports; telling time; months and seasons; ordinal numbers

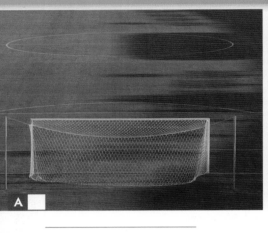

A

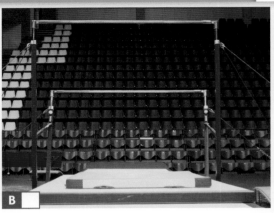

B

C

D 1

READING

1 **Match the sports in the list with the photos. Write 1–4 in the boxes.**

1 ~~golf~~ | 2 gymnastics
3 skateboarding | 4 soccer

2 **Look at Exercise 1. In which sports do you do these actions?**

kick   hit
push   spin
jump   do somersaults

3 🔊 2.02 **Read and listen to the article. Write the names under the photos in Exercise 1.**

Tillman | Xavier
Nikolai | The Firecrackers

4 **Read the article again. Check (✓) the correct box for each sentence.**

	right	wrong	doesn't say
0 Nikolai only uses his feet and legs to stop the ball from falling.		✓	
1 Nikolai can do this for more than a day.			
2 Xavier likes to read golf magazines.			
3 Xavier's hero is Rory McIlroy.			
4 Tillman lives in England.			
5 Tillman doesn't need help to get on the skateboard.			
6 The Firecrackers are a group of friends.			
7 The Firecrackers are very entertaining.			

They're **good!**

Nikolai Kutsenko

Nikolai Kutsenko can do amazing things with a soccer ball. He can kick a ball well, but he can also keep the ball in the air with his feet, legs, and head. Lots of soccer players can do this. But can they do it for 24 hours and 30 minutes without stopping? Nikolai can, and it's a world record!

Xavier Good

Xavier Good is three years old. There are a lot of things this little boy can't do. He can't read or write, for example. But Xavier can do something special. He can hit a golf ball. He can hit it a long way, and he can hit it into the hole. Is he the next Rory McIlroy?

Tillman

Skateboarding is a popular hobby with teenagers everywhere. But in the U.S., people always stop and watch a skateboarder named Tillman. Tillman is an English bulldog, but he can skateboard like a person. He jumps on the skateboard and pushes it with his feet, and he's off!

The Firecrackers

The Firecrackers are a group of young girls who do gymnastics. They can jump and spin and do somersaults like other gymnasts, but the Firecrackers use a jump rope at the same time. Some people call their routine a dance, not a sport, because they use music. But some gymnastics routines use music, too. Everyone agrees that the girls are athletes – and that their routines are fun and amazing to watch.

■ THiNK VALUES ■

The importance of sports

1 **Why do people play sports? Read the reasons below and add two more of your own. Put these reasons in order of importance. Write 1–8 in the boxes.**

- ☐ It's fun.
- ☐ You can make friends.
- ☐ It's good to win.
- ☐ It's easy.
- ☐ It's healthy.
- ☐ It's exciting.
- ☐ _____
- ☐ _____

2 **SPEAKING Compare your ideas with others in the class.**

> *People play sports because they're fun.*

GRAMMAR
can / can't for ability

1 Look at the article on page 67 and complete the sentences. Then complete the rule and the table.

1 They _____ jump.
2 _____ they do it for 24 hours?
3 He _____ read or write.

> **RULE:** We use ¹_____ to talk about ability.
> The negative form is *cannot*. The contracted form is ²_____ .
>
> We don't use *do* or *does* with *can* in questions or negative forms.

Affirmative	Negative
I/You/We/He/She/It/They **can** jump.	I/You/We/He/She/It/They ¹_____ (**cannot**) jump.
Questions	**Short answers**
²_____ I/you/we/he/she/it/they jump?	Yes, I/you/we/he/she/it/they **can**. No, I/you/we/he/she/it/they **can't**.

2 In your notebook, write sentences about John with *can* or *can't*.

0 swim ✓
   John can swim.
1 sing ✗
2 play the guitar ✗
3 play tennis ✓
4 cook ✓
5 speak French ✗
6 dance ✗
7 ride a bike ✓

Pronunciation
The /ɔ/ vowel sound
Go to page 121.

3 Look at the activities in the list. Check (✓) the things you can do.

☐ swim
☐ hit a golf ball
☐ do a somersault
☐ skateboard
☐ throw a ball 20 meters
☐ spell my name in English
☐ count to 20 in English
☐ say the alphabet in less than 30 seconds
☐ read and write
☐ play the guitar
☐ bake a cake
☐ jump high

4 **SPEAKING** Work in pairs. Ask and answer questions.

> *Can you count to 20 in English?*

> *Yes, I can. 1, 2, 3, 4, ...*

Workbook page 64

VOCABULARY
Sports

1 ◀))2.05 Match the words in the list with the photos. Write 1–8 in the boxes. Listen and check.

1 ~~do tae kwon do~~ | 2 ice-skate | 3 play baseball
4 play basketball | 5 play volleyball
6 ride a bike | 7 snowboard | 8 surf

2 **SPEAKING** Work in pairs. Which of these sports *can/can't* you do? Tell your partner.

> *I can ice-skate, but I can't play volleyball.*

Workbook page 67

VOCABULARY
Telling time

1 🔊2.06 Match the times in the list with the clocks. Listen and check.

1 It's three o'clock. | 2 It's half past eight.
3 It's a quarter after ten. | 4 It's a quarter to one.

| A | B | C *1* | D |

2 SPEAKING Write the times under the clocks. Then ask and answer in pairs.

> *What time is it?* *It's a quarter after four.*

0 *It's a quarter after four.* 1 _____

2 _____ 3 _____

> Workbook page 67

LISTENING

1 🔊2.07 Listen to a phone call between Sam and Lucy. When do they decide to go surfing?

2 🔊2.07 Listen again and check (✓) the sports you hear.

	a	tennis
✓	b	surfing
	c	baseball
	d	volleyball
	e	golf
	f	basketball

3 🔊2.07 Listen again. Match the clocks and the sentences. Write 1–8 in the boxes.

1 The volleyball game starts at …
2 The volleyball game ends at …
3 The golf lesson starts at …
4 The golf lesson ends at …
5 It gets dark about …
6 The basketball game ends at …
7 The basketball game starts at …
8 The time now is …

4 Think of four things you do every day. Draw the time that you do them on clocks in your notebook.

5 SPEAKING Work in pairs. Look at your partner's clock. Guess what he/she does at each time. Use the things below or your own ideas.

get up   **eat breakfast**
start school   play soccer   *do your homework*
eat dinner   **go to bed**

> *Do you get up at half past six?*

> *Do you eat breakfast at …?*

> *Do you …?*

■ THiNK SELF-ESTEEM ■

My time: pie chart

1 Look at the example of a pie chart about time then draw one for you.

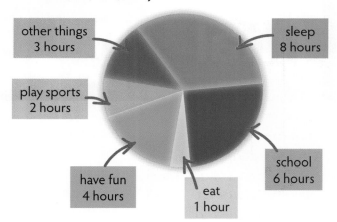

other things 3 hours
sleep 8 hours
play sports 2 hours
school 6 hours
have fun 4 hours
eat 1 hour

2 SPEAKING Work in pairs. Talk about your pie chart.

1 Are you surprised by your chart?
2 Are you happy with how you use your time?
3 Would you like to change? How?

3 SPEAKING Draw your ideal pie chart. Compare with your partner.

| B | C *1* | D |
| A |
| E | F | G | H |

READING

1 SPEAKING **Work in pairs. Discuss these questions.**

1 What important soccer games can you think of?
2 Who are the champions in **a** your country **b** the world?
3 Look at the photos. What do you think is special about this soccer game?

2 ◀》2.08 **Read and listen to the article. Which two teams play "the other final" and who wins?**

_____

_____

3 Read the article again. Put the events in the correct order.

	a	Matthijs organizes a soccer game.
	b	Germany and Brazil play in the World Cup final.
1	c	The Dutch team aren't in the World Cup finals.
	d	Montserrat and Bhutan play a game of soccer.
	e	Matthijs de Jongh has a plan.
	f	The Montserrat national team flies to Bhutan.

4 SPEAKING **Work in pairs. Choose two teams for your perfect "other final."**

1 Where do they play?
2 Who wins?
3 Who scores the goals?

The other final

It's June 30, 2002. In the International Stadium in Yokohama, Japan, two great teams, Brazil and Germany, are ready to play in the World Cup soccer final.

But 4,500 kilometers away in the Changlimithang Stadium in Thimphu, Bhutan, there is another soccer game; Bhutan against Montserrat. Bhutan is number 202 in the world, Montserrat is 203. They are the bottom two teams in the world.

This game is Matthijs de Jongh's idea. He's a Dutch businessman. He can't watch his national team, the Netherlands, because they are not at this World Cup. He's sad, but then he thinks about people from other countries. What about teams that never play in the World Cup? He organizes "the other final" and asks the national teams of Bhutan and Montserrat to play. The Montserrat team flies from the Caribbean to the Himalayan mountains of Bhutan. Thousands of people watch the game. Bhutan wins 4–0, but everyone decides that soccer is the real winner.

After their game, both teams sit down with the rest of the world and enjoy the real World Cup final.

VOCABULARY
Months and seasons

1 **◀))2.09** Put the months in the correct order. Write 1–12 in the boxes. Listen and check.

☐ June	☐ September	☐ February
☐ May	☐ October	☐ July
☐ March	☑ 1 January	☐ August
☐ November	☐ April	☐ December

2 What months are in these seasons in New York City?

winter spring

summer autumn / fall

Workbook page 67

GRAMMAR
Prepositions of time

1 Read the example sentences and complete the rule with *in*, *at*, and *on*.

The soccer game starts **at** 3:00 p.m.
My birthday is **in** March. It's **in** the spring.
The party is **on** Friday.

> **RULE:** With times we use ¹_____ .
> For months and seasons we use ²_____ .
> For days of the week we use ³_____ .

2 **◀))2.10** Do you know when these sporting events are? Guess, then listen and check.

> *The World Cup final is usually in June or July.*

~~The World Cup final~~
The Australian Open Tennis
The World Series of baseball
The Summer Olympics
The Winter Olympics
FIFA Confederations Cup

Workbook page 65

VOCABULARY
Ordinal numbers

1 Look at the article on page 70. Complete the sentence with the missing date.

It's June _____ , 2002. In the International Stadium in Yokohama, …

> **LOOK!** When we say the date, we usually say *March **7th*** or ***the 7th of*** *March*, but we write *March 7*.

2 **◀))2.11** Match the numbers with the words. Listen, check, and repeat.

1st	*h*	9th	☐	**a** sixth		**i** thirtieth
2nd	☐	10th	☐	**b** eleventh		**j** eighth
3rd	☐	11th	☐	**c** thirteenth		**k** thirty-first
4th	☐	12th	☐	**d** third		**l** twelfth
5th	☐	13th	☐	**e** tenth		**m** second
6th	☐	20th	☐	**f** fifth		**n** twentieth
7th	☐	30th	☐	**g** ninth		**o** seventh
8th	☐	31st	☐	**h** first		**p** fourth

3 **SPEAKING** Write three important dates for you. Tell your partner about them.

> *My sister's birthday is on the 8th of May.*

> *Our school's Sports Day is on June 20th.*

Workbook page 67

WRITING
My favorite sportsperson

1 Think of your favorite sportsperson and answer the questions.

1 Who is he/she?
2 Where is he/she from?
3 What sport does he/she do?
4 What sort of things can he/she do?
5 Are there any things he/she can't do?
6 Why do you like him/her?

2 **SPEAKING** Work in pairs. Tell your partner about your favorite sportsperson.

3 Write a short text (50–70 words) about your favorite sportsperson. Use your ideas from Exercises 1 and 2.

The big game

1 **Look at the photos and answer the questions.**

1 Where are they in photo 2?
2 What happens to the TV?

2 🔊 2.12 **Now read and listen to the photostory. Who does Tom want to win?**

TOM The big game is this afternoon at four o'clock. Why don't we all watch it together?
RUBY Great idea!
TOM OK. You call Ellie, and I can call Dan. About 3:30 at my place!
RUBY I have some stuff to do first, but I think 3:30 is OK.

1

2

MAN ON TV Welcome to today's game. We're here live in Rio!
ELLIE It's so exciting.
DAN I know. I love soccer.
TOM The U.S. can win this. I know it. Go U.S.A.!
RUBY No way, Tom. Go Brazil!

3

RUBY Hey. The TV screen. Is it broken? We can't see anything.
ELLIE Where's the game? We want to watch the game!
DAN Come on, Tom. Do something. The game starts in a few minutes!
TOM Just a minute. Let me try and fix it.

4

ELLIE Oh, no. Now the screen's black.
DAN Now what do we do?
TOM It's no big deal. I'm sure I can fix it.
RUBY This is terrible!

DEVELOPING SPEAKING

3 ▣◀ EP4 **Watch to find out how the story continues.**

    1 What sports do Ruby, Ellie, and Dan play?

    2 Who wins the game on TV?

4 ▣◀ EP4 **Watch again. Choose the correct answers.**

    0 Who offers to help Tom?

       Ⓐ Dan

       B Ruby

       C Ellie

    1 Where is the table for table tennis?

       A in the living room

       B in Tom's bedroom

       C in the game room

    2 Who wins at table tennis?

       A Dan

       B Ruby

       C Ellie

    3 Where is the basketball hoop?

       A in the garage

       B in the yard

       C in the park

    4 Where does Tom find the others?

       A in the kitchen

       B in the living room

       C in the yard

    5 Who wins the big game?

       A the U.S.

       B Brazil

       C We don't know.

PHRASES FOR FLUENCY

1 **Find the expressions 1–4 in the story. Who says them?**

    1 stuff

    _____

    2 Now what …?

    _____

    3 It's no big deal.

    _____

    4 I'm sure …

    _____

2 **How do you say the expressions in Exercise 1 in your language?**

3 **Put the sentences in the correct order to make a dialogue.**

☐	ANDY	You know, books and things. I need them for school. Now what do I do?
☐	ANDY	No books? Are you sure I can do that?
1	ANDY	Oh, no! I don't have my school stuff with me.
☐	SUE	What school stuff?
☐	SUE	Oh, it's no big deal. You can go to class without your books.
☐	SUE	Yes, I'm sure you can. Come on, we're late.

4 **Complete the mini-dialogues with the expressions from Exercise 1.**

    0 A Who is that woman?

       B ___*I'm sure*___ she's a famous actress, but I can't remember her name.

    1 A Come to the store with me.

       B I can't. I have a lot of _____ to do at home.

    2 A My computer's broken.

       B But we need the Internet! _____ ?

    3 A I can't find my pen.

       B _____ I have an extra one. Here you go.

FUNCTIONS
Making suggestions

1 **Complete the sentences from the story. Use the words and phrases in the list.**

How about | Let's | Why don't

    1 _____ we all watch it together?

    2 _____ play table tennis!

    3 _____ another game?

2 **Complete the suggestions.**

    1 A I'm bored.

       B _____ watching a movie?

    2 A There's nothing to do.

       B _____ we go for a hike?

    3 A I'm hungry.

       B _____ make some sandwiches.

3 SPEAKING **Work in pairs. Act out the mini-dialogues in Exercise 2.**

4 SPEAKING **Make two new dialogues. Use these words for speaker A.**

thirsty
tired

DANCE TO THE MUSIC

READING

1 Match the words in the list with the photos. Write 1–5 in the boxes.

1 a concert | 2 a musician | 3 a singer
4 a trumpet | 5 a violin

2 Look at the photos on page 75. They show a concert. Where is it happening?

- 1 in a train station
- 2 in a concert hall
- 3 in a supermarket
- 4 in a school

3 Do you use Twitter? What do you know about Tweets?

4 ◀)) 2.13 Read and listen to the Tweets. Answer the questions.

0 How does Alex feel at 09:44? (Hint: look at his hashtag.)
bored

1 How many musicians are playing at 09:48?
2 How do the people in the supermarket feel at 09:49?
3 How many people are singing in the concert at 09:50?
4 How does Alex feel at 09:51?
5 What are the musicians doing at 09:55?

A

B

C 1

D

E

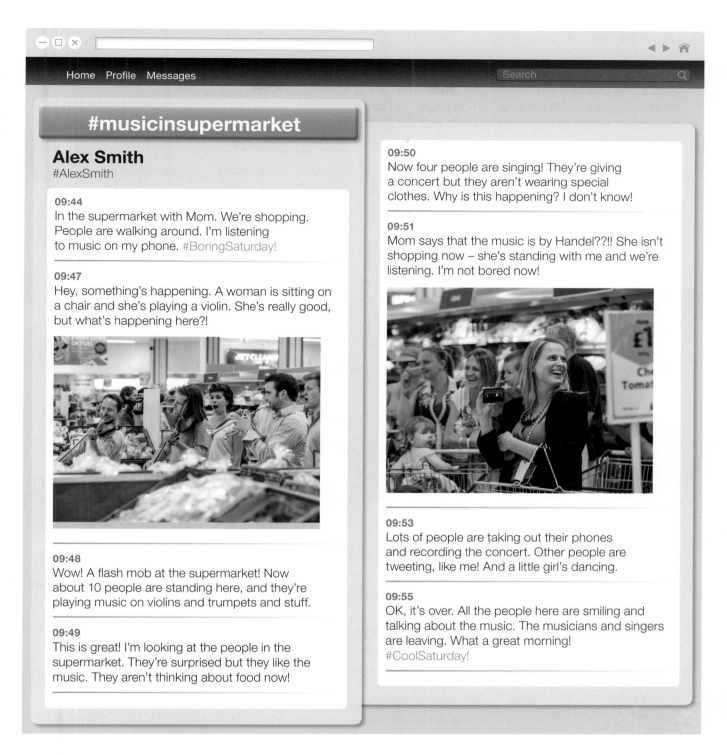

#musicinsupermarket

Alex Smith
#AlexSmith

09:44
In the supermarket with Mom. We're shopping. People are walking around. I'm listening to music on my phone. #BoringSaturday!

09:47
Hey, something's happening. A woman is sitting on a chair and she's playing a violin. She's really good, but what's happening here?!

09:48
Wow! A flash mob at the supermarket! Now about 10 people are standing here, and they're playing music on violins and trumpets and stuff.

09:49
This is great! I'm looking at the people in the supermarket. They're surprised but they like the music. They aren't thinking about food now!

09:50
Now four people are singing! They're giving a concert but they aren't wearing special clothes. Why is this happening? I don't know!

09:51
Mom says that the music is by Handel??!! She isn't shopping now – she's standing with me and we're listening. I'm not bored now!

09:53
Lots of people are taking out their phones and recording the concert. Other people are tweeting, like me! And a little girl's dancing.

09:55
OK, it's over. All the people here are smiling and talking about the music. The musicians and singers are leaving. What a great morning! #CoolSaturday!

■ THiNK VALUES ■

Music

1 **SPEAKING** Check (✓) the places where you listen to music. Tell your partner. How many are the same?

☐ in my room	☐ on the bus/train
☐ outside	☐ at concerts
☐ at school	☐ another place (Where?)

> *I listen to music in my room, outside, and on the bus.*

2 What's important for you about music? Write 1–3 in the boxes: 3 = very important, 2 = important, 1 = not important.

☐ It makes me happy.

☐ I can listen with friends.

☐ It's free.

☐ I can forget my problems.

☐ I can dance to it.

3 **SPEAKING** Work in groups. Compare your ideas.

GRAMMAR
Present continuous

1 Look at the examples of the present continuous. Underline other examples in the reading text on page 75. Then circle the correct words to complete the rule and the table.

I'**m listening** to music on my phone.
A woman **is sitting** on a chair.
They **aren't wearing** special clothes.
What's **happening**?

> **RULE:** We use the present continuous to talk about things that [1]*happen every day / are happening now*. We form the present continuous with the present tense of [2]*be / have* and the *-ing* form of the main verb.

Affirmative	Negative	Question + short answer
I'**m** (**am**) listen**ing**.	I'**m not** (**am not**) listen**ing**.	[5]_____ I listen**ing**? Yes, I [6]_____ . No, I'**m not**.
You/We/They [1]_____ (**are**) listen**ing**.	You/We/They **aren't** (**are not**) [3]_____ .	[7]_____ you/we/they listen**ing**? Yes, you/we/they **are**. No, you/we/they [8]_____ .
He/She/It [2]_____ (**is**) listen**ing**.	He/She/It [4]_____ (**is not**) listen**ing**.	[9]_____ he/she/it [10]_____ ? Yes, he/she/it [11]_____ . No, he/she/it **isn't**.

2 Look at the pictures. Then write a name to complete the sentences.

0 __Jake__ is singing.
1 _____ are sitting.
2 _____ is taking a picture.
3 _____ is talking on the phone.
4 _____ is leaving.
5 _____ is reading.
6 _____ are dancing.
7 _____ is standing and cheering.
8 _____ is wearing a blue hat and smiling.
9 _____ is running.

> **LOOK!** Spelling
> si**ng** – sing**ing**   liv**e** – liv**ing**
> sw**im** – swi**mming**

3 Write the correct *-ing* form of these verbs.

0 come   *coming*
1 take   _____
2 get   _____
3 shop   _____
4 bake   _____
5 watch   _____
6 play   _____
7 study   _____

4 Complete the sentences with the verbs from Exercise 3 in the correct form.

0 **A** Come on, Jane, we're late!
  B OK, Sam, I *'m coming* now!
1 **A** Where's Molly?
  B She's in the living room. She _____ TV.
2 **A** Is Jacob here?
  B No, he isn't. He _____ computer games in his bedroom.
3 **A** Can I talk to Mike, please?
  B Sorry, he's at the mall. He _____ .
4 **A** Let's go home now.
  B You're right. It _____ late. Look, it's almost ten o'clock.
5 **A** Is your dad in the kitchen?
  B Yes, he is! He _____ a cake!
6 **A** Where are Alex and Emma?
  B They _____ the dog for a walk in the park.
7 **A** So, your sister is in college?
  B That's right. She _____ medicine.

Workbook page 72

Sally

Linda   Greg

Jake
Olive   Paola   Steve

David

Kelly

Julie   Mike

LISTENING

1 Look at the different dances in the photos. Where do you think they come from? Choose from the countries in the list.

Brazil | China | Greece | Indonesia
Spain | Thailand | Turkey

2 In which photos can you see these things? Write 1–4 in the boxes.

1   A man is playing a guitar and a woman is dancing.
2   The men are wearing clothes of different colors.
3   The men and the women are dancing in a line.
4   The men are wearing black-and-white cloths around their bodies.

3 🔊 2.14 Listen to the program. Which three photos in Exercise 1 do the people talk about?

4 🔊 2.14 Listen again and choose the correct options.

0   Janie's family goes to *Spain* / *Turkey* every year.
1   Janie loves the clothes that the *men* / *women* wear.
2   The dancers in Turkey wear skirts that are *the same color* / *different colors.*
3   The dancers in Turkey don't *have any music* / *stop.*
4   In the Kecak dance, there isn't any *music* / *moving.*
5   The Kecak dance is only by *men* / *musicians.*

5 Imagine you can go and watch one of the dances. Which dance do you want to watch?

FUNCTIONS
Describing a scene

1 Match 1–3 with a–c.

When we describe a scene, we often use:

1   the present continuous ☐
2   prepositions ☐
3   adjectives ☐

a   for colors, sizes, etc.
b   to say what people are doing.
c   to say where people and things are.

2 Read the text and answer the questions.

1   Which photo in Listening Exercise 1 is this person describing?
2   Underline examples of the language mentioned in Exercise 1 (present continuous, prepositions, adjectives).

> There are lots of people. One woman is dancing. She's wearing a red dress. There are some musicians behind her. They're playing music. Two people are sitting on chairs. They are watching and clapping. Everyone is happy. They're enjoying the music and the dancing.

3 **SPEAKING** Look at the picture. Work in pairs. Describe the scene.

READING

1 🔊 2.15 **Read and listen to the dialogue and look at the picture. Who is Andy?**

EMILY	Hi, Mike. Are you enjoying the party?
MIKE	Hey, Emily. Yeah, it's OK, but I don't like the music.
EMILY	Oh, really? I like the music. Hey! Come and dance! I really like dancing!
MIKE	No, thanks. I don't like dancing very much. Ask Andy to dance with you. He's a really good dancer.
EMILY	Andy? Who's Andy?
MIKE	He's over there. Look – he's wearing gray pants and a green shirt. Can you see him?
EMILY	Oh, yes, I can see him. A green shirt!! Ugh!
MIKE	Oh, it's just a shirt! Go and ask him to dance.
EMILY	No. I hate talking to boys.
MIKE	But you're talking to me.
EMILY	I know, but you're my friend. That's different. I don't know Andy. And he's wearing a green shirt!
MIKE	You're crazy. Andy is really nice. He loves going to parties, and dancing and meeting new people. Oh, look, he's coming over here.
ANDY	Hi. I'm Andy.
EMILY	Oh, hi. I'm Emily. Do you like dancing?
ANDY	Yes, I love it! Do you want to dance?
EMILY	OK! I like your shirt!
MIKE	What? Wow. I really don't understand girls!

2 **Read the dialogue again and complete the sentences.**

0 Mike is enjoying the party but
   he doesn't like the music .

1 Andy is wearing _____ .

2 Emily doesn't like _____ .

3 Emily and Mike are _____ .

GRAMMAR
like / don't like + -ing

1 **Complete the sentences from the dialogue in Reading Exercise 1. Then complete the rule.**

0 Come and dance! I really like *dancing* !
1 I hate _____ to boys.
2 He loves _____ to parties.
3 Do you like _____ ?

> **RULE:** We use the verbs (*don't*) *like* / _____ / *hate* + verb + *-ing* to give opinions about activities.

2 **Write *like*, *don't like*, *love*, and *hate* in the correct places.**

🙂🙂 1 _____
🙂   2 _____
🙁   3 _____
🙁🙁 4 _____

3 **Complete the sentences. Use *like*, *don't like*, *love*, or *hate* and the correct form of the verb.**

0 I ___*love watching*___ sports on TV.
   🙂🙂 (watch)
1 I _____ to the movies. 🙁 (go)
2 I _____ early. 🙁🙁 (get up)
3 My family _____ on vacation.
   🙂 (go)
4 My best friend _____ .
   🙂🙂 (run)
5 My parents _____ . 🙁 (dance)
6 _____ your father
   _____ ? 🙂 (cook)

4 **Look at the sentences in Exercise 3. Which are true for you? Change the ones that are not true for you.**

Workbook page 73

VOCABULARY
Clothes

1 ▣2.16 **Match the names of the clothes with the pictures. Write 1–12 in the boxes. Listen and check.**

1 a dress | 2 a coat | 3 jeans | 4 a sweater
5 a shirt | 6 shoes | 7 shorts | 8 a skirt
9 socks | 10 a T-shirt | 11 sneakers | 12 pants

Paul

Anna

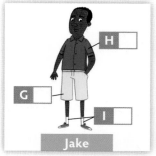

Jake

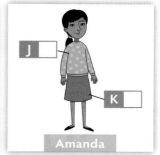

Amanda

Simon

2 **Look at the pictures in Exercise 1 again. What are the people wearing?**

0 Paul is wearing
   blue jeans, a white T-shirt, and sneakers .
1 Anna is wearing _____ .
2 Jake _____ .
3 Amanda _____ .
4 Simon _____ .

3 SPEAKING **Work in pairs. Ask and answer the questions.**

1 What clothes do you love wearing? What clothes do you hate wearing?
2 Do you like shopping for clothes? Why or why not?
3 What is your teacher wearing today?
4 Which colors do you love or hate wearing?

> *I love wearing jeans and sneakers but I hate wearing shoes and pants.*

Workbook page 75 ▶

Pronunciation
Intonation: listing items
Go to page 121. ◀》

■ TRAIN TO THINK ■
Memorizing

1 **Look at the picture for two minutes.**

2 SPEAKING **Student A: Go to page 127. Student B: Go to page 128. Listen to the questions your partner asks and answer with short answers. Correct the negative answers.**

Culture

Musical instruments around the world

HOME   ABOUT   NEWS   CONTACT

1

The berimbau

This is a Brazilian instrument. It's made of wood. It's long and thin and has one string. You play the berimbau by hitting the string with a stick. Musicians play the berimbau when people dance *capoeira*. Capoeira is now famous in many parts of the world, not only in Brazil.

A ☐

Brazil

2

The didgeridoo

The didgeridoo is a famous musical instrument that comes from Australia. It's like a big, long trumpet, but it's made of wood. You blow into it, and it makes a very unusual deep sound. Didgeridoos are difficult to hold because they are one to three meters long. The musician usually puts the didgeridoo on the ground.

B ☐

Australia

3

The bonang

The bonang is a group of round, metal pots. Musicians play these in Indonesia in an orchestra of many musicians. They put the pots together in lines. Then they hit the pots with a stick that has a piece of cloth around it. All the pots are different sizes so they all make different sounds. Some people say that the sound is very relaxing.

C ☐

Indonesia

1 Look at the photos on page 80. Find these things.

blow | a piece of cloth
an orchestra | the ground
a stick | wood

2 ◀)) 2.19 Read and listen to the article. Which countries do these instruments come from?

3 Read the article again. Mark the sentences T (true) or F (false).

0 There is only one string on a berimbau.	T
1 Capoeira is the music that you play on the berimbau.	
2 A didgeridoo is like a trumpet.	
3 Didgeridoos are always the same size.	
4 The bonang has one pot.	
5 You play the bonang using a stick.	

4 **SPEAKING** Are there any special musical instruments in your country? Can you play any musical instruments? Tell the class.

WRITING
Describing a scene

1 Read these three Tweets and look at the photos. Where is Sandra? Check (✓) the correct photo.

2 Read the Tweets again. <u>Underline</u> examples of the present continuous tense.

3 Write notes to describe how you are feeling in each of these situations.

1 You're at a bus stop. It's raining. You're going to meet friends and then go and see a local band play. The bus doesn't come.

2 You're at home. The weather outside is very nice and you want to go out, but you can't. You have to study.

3 You're at home. You're watching a very good movie. You want to tell your friends that it's really good.

4 Write three Tweets for each situation in Exercise 3.

Remember:

● A Tweet can only be 140 characters (including spaces).

● You can say something in your second and third Tweet about how the situation is changing.

3:22
Here we are. We're waiting. I think there are 3,000 people here! It's fantastic. People are singing and smiling – great! #Excited4MyBoys

3:28
I think they're coming out. Yes – they're here! Everyone is shouting and cheering!! The people in the band are smiling, they're very happy.

3: 49
They're playing my favorite song! Everyone's smiling and singing. I'm watching my favorite band – this is the best! #BestNightEver

A

B

■ THiNK EXAMS ■

LISTENING
Part 1: Multiple-choice pictures

1 🔊2.20 **You will hear five short conversations. There is one question for each conversation. For each question, choose the right answer (A, B, or C).**

0 What time does Rob get home from school?

A ☐   B ✓   C ☐

3 Which instrument does Mike play?

A ☐   B ☐   C ☐

1 When is Kim's birthday?

A ☐   B ☐   C ☐

4 Which of Jessica's clothes does Luke like?

A ☐   B ☐   C ☐

2 What is Lidia's favorite month?

A ☐   B ☐   C ☐

READING AND WRITING
Part 6: Word completion

2 **Read the descriptions of some words about sports. What is the word for each one? The first letter is already there. There is one space for each other letter in the word.**

0 You ride this. It has two wheels.

b i c y c l e

1 You do this in white clothes.

t _ _ _ k _ _ _ _ _ _

2 You need snow to do this.

s _ _ _ _ _ _ _ _

3 You play this on a team of six people.

v _ _ _ _ _ _ _ _ _

4 You do this in water.

s _ _ _

5 In this sport, you throw a ball through a hoop.

b _ _ _ _ _ _ _ _ _ _

TEST YOURSELF

VOCABULARY

1 **Complete the sentences with the words in the list. There are two extra words.**

baseball | cheering | coat | doing | fourth | making
sitting | sneakers | studying | surf | taking | three

1 It's cold outside! Put a _____ on when you go out.
2 I love playing _____ .
3 We like _____ under the big tree in the backyard on hot summer days.
4 I'm in the kitchen. I'm _____ sandwiches for the party.
5 My brother is going to college in Australia. He's _____ math there.
6 You can't wear _____ to a party! Wear your new shoes!
7 My sister's at the gym. She's _____ tae kwon do.
8 I love _____ pictures of different sporting events. Look at this one!
9 Thanksgiving? In the U.S., it's the _____ Thursday in November.
10 They're winning! Everyone is _____ !

/10

GRAMMAR

2 **Complete the sentences with the words in the box.**

can | can't | don't | like | stand | standing

1 Do you _____ reading magazines?
2 I don't like _____ on the bus.
3 I'm sick. I _____ go out today.
4 I don't want to sit down. I can _____ and watch. It's OK.
5 We really _____ like going for hikes in winter.
6 He _____ run 100 meters in twelve seconds.

3 **Find and correct the mistake in each sentence.**

1 He can to count to 20 in Japanese. _____
2 Please be quiet. I'm study for the test tomorrow. _____
3 She doesn't can speak English. _____
4 I don't like watch sports. _____
5 She's downtown right now. She shops. _____
6 Do you can play the piano? _____

/12

FUNCTIONAL LANGUAGE

4 **Write the missing words.**

1 A _____ time is it?
  B It's three _____ . I'm bored!
  A Me too. Why _____ we play a game?
  B A game? No, thanks. _____ about going for a hike?
2 A Look at those people! They're _____ very strange clothes.
  B Yes, they're going to a big party in the park. It's Sunday today!
  A What _____ does the party start?
  B Two o'clock. Oh, look. It's a quarter _____ two now! _____ go and join them.

/8

MY SCORE   /30

| 22 – 30 |
| 10 – 21 |
| 0 – 9 |

A

C

D

B

E

F

G

H *1*

READING

1 **Look at the photos. Where can you see the words in the list? Write 1–8 in the boxes.**

1 a carrot cake | 2 a chef
3 a plate | 4 cooking
5 an omelette | 6 tomato soup
7 a salad | 8 a steak

2 **SPEAKING** **What other food words do you know?**

> Pizza, apples, hamburgers, …

3 **SPEAKING** **Tell your partner what food you like and don't like.**

> I like … . I don't like … .

4 **Look at the photos on page 85. What is unusual about the chefs? Read and check.**

5 **◄))2.21** **Read and listen to the article again. Mark the sentences T (true), F (false), or D (doesn't say).**

0 Billy is ten years old and he's from New York. — *T*
1 He wants to be a star chef.
2 His sister likes cooking, too, but she's not very good.
3 The other children on the TV show aren't very good cooks.
4 Children must be ten years old to be on *Star Junior Chefs*.
5 The chefs' hands must be clean.
6 It's OK for the children to eat the food they are cooking.
7 After the TV show Billy goes home to study.

Young kitchen stars

Billy doesn't want to be a star chef when he's 20. He wants to be one now. This is why he's on the *Star Junior Chefs* TV show.

The ten-year-old New Yorker likes cooking. He can make fantastic soups and salads, excellent omelettes, and the best cakes. But there are many other children on the show, too. And they are all very good cooks.

More and more young people are interested in cooking. Many of them learn it from their parents. Others watch special cooking videos for children on YouTube. In many cities, there are special cooking classes for young people. Some of them are for children as young as three years old!

The show starts. Billy is excited. He knows he's an excellent cook. This time he makes tomato soup, some salad, steak, and carrot cake. The experts in the studio love Billy's food, and he stays on the show.

It's 5:00 p.m. The show is over. Billy is happy and a little tired. He goes home. He has a deal with his parents. He can be on the show, but he must do his homework, too.

But what must you do to become a star chef? Of course, it's important that you like cooking and are really good at it, but there are some rules. You must be nine years old or older to be on *Star Junior Chefs*. "We must wash our hands before we start cooking," Billy says. "And of course we must not put them in our mouths. A chef doesn't do that! And we must be very careful with hot plates."

■ THiNK VALUES ■

How you eat is important

1 SPEAKING How often do you do these things? Write *always, sometimes, often,* or *never.* Then tell the class.

- [ ] a eat slowly _____
- [ ] b eat with other people _____
- [ ] c sit at a table to eat _____
- [ ] d eat very fast _____
- [ ] e eat alone _____
- [ ] f eat and play computer games at the same time _____

> I always eat slowly. I sometimes eat with other people.

2 Look again at the things in Exercise 1. Are they good things to do? Write 1–3 in the boxes: 1 = a good thing to do, 2 = an OK thing to do, 3 = a bad thing to do.

3 SPEAKING Compare your ideas with a partner.

> I often eat …

> I think … is good.

> I think … is not so good.

GRAMMAR
must / must not

1 Complete the sentences from the article on page 85 with *must* or *must not*. Then complete the rule.

1 You _____ be nine years old or older to be on *Star Junior Chefs*.

2 We _____ wash our hands before we start cooking.

3 We _____ put them in our mouths.

> **RULE:** We use *must* (*not*) to talk about rules.
> Use ¹_____ to say that it's necessary to do something.
> Use ²_____ to say that it's not OK to do something.

2 Complete the mini-dialogues. Use *must* or *must not* + a verb from the list.

eat | forget | give | go

0 A Hey, can I borrow this book?
　B Sure, but you ___*must give*___ it back next week.

1 A Mom, can I have some chocolate?
　B Of course not! You know you _____ chocolate. It makes you sick.

2 A Julia's birthday is tomorrow.
　B That's right. We _____ to buy her a gift today.

3 A Oh, no. There isn't any milk.
　B I _____ to the store after work. We're out of everything!

3 SPEAKING Work in pairs. Think of some things that are important for you to do (or things you really can't forget to do) in the next few days.

> I must write an email to my friend Mark.

> I must not forget to clean my room.

Workbook page 82

VOCABULARY
Food and drink

1 ◀》2.22 Write the names of the food and drinks under the photos. Listen and check.

2 SPEAKING Which word in each group is different? Why?

1 coffee – potato – tea
2 banana – orange – sausage
3 carrot – chicken – beef
4 milk – strawberry – apple
5 pepper – potato – hamburger (burger)

> Number 1 is potatoes — coffee and tea are drinks.

3 SPEAKING Look at the food words in Exercise 1. Work in pairs. Ask and answer questions to find three things you both like.

> Do you like tomatoes?

> Yes, I love them. What about you?

> I like them. Do you like ...?

Workbook page 85

Meat

0 *chicken*　1 _____　2 _____　3 _____

Fruit

4 _____　5 _____　6 _____　7 _____

Vegetables

8 _____　9 _____　10 _____　11 _____

Drinks

12 _____　13 _____　14 _____　15 _____

LISTENING

1 Look at the picture. What's happening?

2 🔊 2.23 Listen to the dialogue. What is Raul cooking? Does he eat it?

3 🔊 2.23 Listen again. Put the sentences in the order you hear them. Write 1–6 in the boxes.

	a	Can I clean the kitchen later?
1	**b**	Can I make an omelette?
	c	Can I come into the kitchen now?
	d	I must be quick now.
	e	Would you like some help?
	f	Can I go to the pizza place?

GRAMMAR
can (asking for permission)

1 Match these answers to the questions in Listening Exercise 3. Then read the rule.

1 OK, but don't forget to do it. ☐
2 No, wait, Mom. ☐
3 Yes, you can. ☐

> **RULE:** We use *can* + subject …? to ask if it's OK to do something.

2 🔊 2.24 Complete the questions with *can* and a verb from the list. Listen and check.

~~do~~ | eat | go out | play | try on | use

0 __Can__ I __do__ my homework later?
1 _____ I _____ these jeans, please?
2 _____ I _____ your laptop, please?
3 Dad, _____ I _____ tonight?
4 _____ we _____ baseball in the backyard?
5 _____ we _____ dinner in front of the TV?

3 Match the answers with the questions in Exercise 2.

0	**a**	No, you can't. Do it now.
	b	Of course you can. But be careful.
	c	No you can't, you have school tomorrow.
	d	Sorry, I need it to write some emails.
	e	Yes, the changing room is over there.
	f	Well, OK. It's your birthday.

Workbook pages 82–83 ▸

■ THiNK SELF-ESTEEM ■
You are what you eat

1 Think about what is true for you. Circle 1–5: 1 = certainly true, 5 = certainly not true.

1	I often eat between meals.	1 – 2 – 3 – 4 – 5
2	I always eat breakfast.	1 – 2 – 3 – 4 – 5
3	I eat fruit and vegetables every day.	1 – 2 – 3 – 4 – 5
4	I drink lots of water.	1 – 2 – 3 – 4 – 5
5	I eat a lot of candy.	1 – 2 – 3 – 4 – 5
6	I brush my teeth after every meal.	1 – 2 – 3 – 4 – 5

2 **SPEAKING** Compare your answers with a partner.

I often eat between meals.

I eat fruit every day.

READING

1 Read the menu. What would you choose to eat?

2 🔊 2.25 Read and listen to the dialogue. What doesn't Jack like? _____

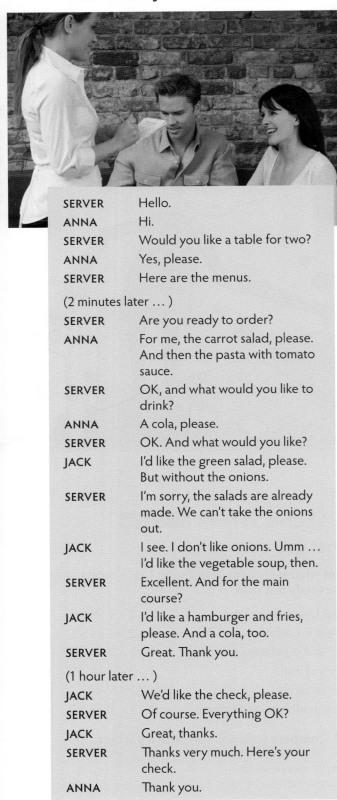

SERVER	Hello.
ANNA	Hi.
SERVER	Would you like a table for two?
ANNA	Yes, please.
SERVER	Here are the menus.

(2 minutes later …)

SERVER	Are you ready to order?
ANNA	For me, the carrot salad, please. And then the pasta with tomato sauce.
SERVER	OK, and what would you like to drink?
ANNA	A cola, please.
SERVER	OK. And what would you like?
JACK	I'd like the green salad, please. But without the onions.
SERVER	I'm sorry, the salads are already made. We can't take the onions out.
JACK	I see. I don't like onions. Umm … I'd like the vegetable soup, then.
SERVER	Excellent. And for the main course?
JACK	I'd like a hamburger and fries, please. And a cola, too.
SERVER	Great. Thank you.

(1 hour later …)

JACK	We'd like the check, please.
SERVER	Of course. Everything OK?
JACK	Great, thanks.
SERVER	Thanks very much. Here's your check.
ANNA	Thank you.

3 **Read the dialogue again. What does Anna order? What does Jack order?**

Zoe's café

Menu

Our appetizers

Carrot salad	$5.25
Green salad (with onion and tomato)	$7.50
Vegetable soup	$6.60

Our main courses

Steak	$15.80
Pasta with tomato sauce	$8.50
Fish and chips	$8.50
Hamburger and fries	$7.80
Chicken and tomato sandwich	$6.50
Sausage pizza	$5.20

Our desserts

Ice cream (per scoop)	$1.20

Vanilla, strawberry, lemon, and chocolate

Our drinks

Juice (orange or apple)	$1.90
Cola	$1.70
Coffee	$2.20
Tea	$1.60
Water	$1.10

4 **Who says these things in a restaurant? Write S (server) or G (guest) in the boxes.**

0 Can I help you? **S**

1 A table for two, please. ☐

2 Here are the menus. ☐

3 Are you ready to order? ☐

4 What would you like to drink? ☐

5 I'd like the vegetable soup, then. ☐

6 Can we have the check, please? ☐

7 Would you like a dessert? ☐

GRAMMAR
I'd like … / Would you like …?

1 Complete these sentences from the dialogue on page 88. Then complete the rule.

1 Would you _____ a table for two?
2 _____ like the vegetable soup.
3 What _____ you like to drink?
4 _____ like the check, please.

> **RULE:** We use I + would ('d) + [1]_____ to ask for something in a nice way.
> We use Would + you + [2]_____ ? to offer something.

2 How do you say *I'd like …* and *Would you like …?* in your language?

3 In your notebook, put the words in the correct order to make sentences or questions.

0 like / a / I'd / please / banana,
I'd like a banana, please.
1 like / some / you / Would / coffee / ?
2 like / a hamburger / I'd / and / please / fries,
3 you / What / to / would / like / eat / ?
4 to / We'd / like / here / sit
5 would / this afternoon / What / you / like / to / do / ?

4 Complete what the people are saying.

1 _____ order now?
2 _____ some coffee?
3 We _____ sit there, please.
4 I _____ some ice cream, please.

5 SPEAKING Work in groups. One of you is the server at Zoe's café, the others order food and drinks. Act out the situation. Use the sentences in Reading Exercise 4 and Grammar Exercise 3 to help you.

> Workbook page 83

> **Pronunciation**
> Intonation: giving two choices
> Go to page 121.

VOCABULARY
Meals

1 ◁》2.28 Match the words in the list to the items in the picture. Write 1–9 in the boxes. Listen and check.

1 ~~bread~~ | 2 butter | 3 cereal | 4 egg | 5 fruit
6 honey | 7 jam | 8 toast | 9 yogurt

2 SPEAKING Make a table like this in your notebook for breakfast, lunch, and dinner. Write down things you eat and drink. Compare charts with a partner.

	always	often	sometimes	never
breakfast				

> For breakfast I always drink …

> I never have (any) … for lunch.

> Workbook page 85

WRITING
A meal plan for your friend

1 Ask a partner to give you his/her table from Vocabulary Exercise 2. Imagine he/she is staying at your home for the weekend. You want to make meals that he/she likes. Write a menu for him/her.

2 Show your ideas to your partner. Is he/she happy with the meals?

Saturday	Sunday
Breakfast:	Breakfast:
Lunch:	Lunch:
Dinner:	Dinner:

The pizza

1 **Look at the photos and answer the questions.**

1 Who can you see in the photos?
2 Where are they and what are they doing?

2 ◀))2.29 **Now read and listen to the photostory. What does Ruby hate?**

DAD So what are you doing, boys?
DAN Tom is making pizza for the girls, and I'm helping him.
TOM Is that OK, Dad?
DAD Of course. No problem. You make great pizza! What time do they get here?
TOM Six o'clock. We have half an hour.

1

DAD Do you want some help, Tom?
TOM No, I'm OK, thanks. OK, first we need to add the tomato sauce.
DAN Can I cut the peppers for you?
TOM OK.
DAD Just be careful with the knife.

2

TOM What are you doing, Dad?
DAD I'm putting a little cheese on the pizza.
TOM Don't do that!
DAD Too late.

3

DAD It's only cheese.
DAN The thing is, Ruby hates cheese.
DAD She hates cheese? Oh, dear.
TOM Now what?
DAN We can't make another one. We don't have time.
TOM What can we do?

4

DEVELOPING SPEAKING

3 ▣◀ **EP5** **Watch to find out how the story continues.**

1 Who does Tom's dad call?

2 Why are the boys surprised?

4 ▣◀ **EP5** **Watch again. Put the events in order. Write 1–6 in the boxes.**

☐	a	The food from Andy's Chicken House arrives.
☐	b	The girls eat the pizza.
☐	c	The boys try and take the girls to the living room.
1	d	Tom's dad calls Andy's Chicken House.
☐	e	The girls arrive.
☐	f	The girls say hello to Tom's dad.

PHRASES FOR FLUENCY

1 **Find the expressions 1–4 in the story. Who says them?**

1 Of course. _____

2 be careful … _____

3 a little … _____

4 The thing is, … _____

2 **How do you say the expressions in Exercise 1 in your language?**

3 **Put the sentences in the correct order to make a dialogue.**

☐	GREG	Well, I really want some lasagna. But the thing is, I don't know how to make it.
1	GREG	Do you like Italian food?
☐	GREG	Yeah, I don't know how to cook very well.
☐	NADIA	Oh. And you need a little help?
☐	NADIA	Of course. I love spaghetti and stuff. Why?
☐	NADIA	Well, you can use my mom's cookbook. But be careful – she loves that book!

4 **Complete the dialogues with the expressions from Exercise 1.**

1 A Let's go to the movies tonight.

B No, thanks. I'm feeling _____ sick.

A Really? Oh, no. Do you want some help?

B Actually, that isn't true. I'm sorry. _____ , I don't have any money.

2 A Can I look at your new phone?

B _____ . Here it is.

A Oh, it's really nice!

B Thanks, I love it. Oh, _____ ! Don't break it!

FUNCTIONS
Offering to help

1 **Look at the photostory again. Who says these expressions?**

1 Do you want some help? _____

2 Can I cut the peppers for you? _____

2 **Match the possible answers to the sentences in Exercise 1.**

a	OK. Thanks!	1
b	Yes, please.	☐
c	Sure. Here's a knife you can use.	☐
d	No, I'm OK, thanks.	☐

3 **Work in pairs. Write a short dialogue for each picture. Use expressions from Exercises 1 and 2.**

4 **SPEAKING** **Act out your dialogues.**

10 | HIGH FLIERS

READING

1 Match the words in the list with the photos. Write 1–6 in the boxes.

1 achievements | 2 astronaut | 3 factory
4 spacecraft | 5 skydiving | 6 stamps

2 Look at the photos and answer the questions.

1 What are the names of the two people?
2 Where were they from?
3 Why are they famous?

3 Name some famous people in your country. Why are they famous?

4 ◀)) 2.30 Read and listen to the article and answer the question.

Why is Valentina Tereshkova famous?

5 Read the article again and put the events in order.

	a	Tereshkova was in space for three days.
	b	She was named "Woman of the Century."
	c	She was a carrier of the Olympic flag.
	d	There was a competition to find new astronauts.
1	e	Valentina Tereshkova was born.

B 1

C

A

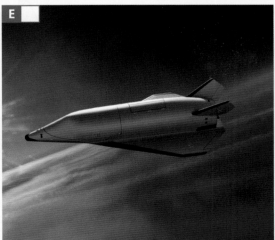

D

E

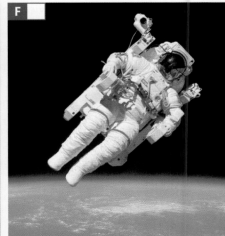

F

It was her dream to be an astronaut

Valentina Tereshkova was the first woman in space.

She was born in Russia on March 6, 1937. Her father was a driver, and her mother was a factory worker. Valentina was a worker in a factory, too. Her hobby was skydiving, and it was her dream to be an astronaut and go into space.

In 1962, there was a big competition to find new astronauts. There were 400 people interested in going into space. The training program wasn't very easy, but Valentina was the lucky one. Her big day was June 16, 1963, and she was ready.

The name of Valentina's spacecraft was Vostok 6. The flight was very difficult because there were many technical problems, and she wasn't very well for most of the flight. She was in space for three days. She is the only woman in history to do a solo space flight.

After Valentina's time in space she was very famous all over the world. Her face was on stamps in several countries.

In the year 2000, there was a big celebration in London, and Valentina Tereshkova was named the "Woman of the Century."

At the opening ceremony of the Winter Olympics in Russia in 2014, Valentina Tereshkova was one of the carriers of the Olympic flag.

These moments were very important to her. Valentina Tereshkova is proud of her achievements.

▮THiNK VALUES▮

Hard work and achievement

1 In 2000, Valentina Tereshkova was named "Woman of the Century." Which of the following, do you think, were important for her success? Write N (not important) or I (important).

1 She was born in 1937. ☐
2 Her father was a driver. ☐
3 She was a factory worker. ☐
4 It was her dream to be an astronaut and go into space. ☐
5 She was lucky. ☐
6 The flight was difficult, but Tereshkova was strong. ☐
7 She was in space for three days. ☐

2 SPEAKING Compare your answers with a partner. Do you agree?

> She was born in 1937. I think that was important for her success because it was the start of air travel.

> I agree. / I don't agree. I think …

GRAMMAR
Simple past: *be* (affirmative and negative)

1 **Complete the sentences from the text on page 93. Then complete the rule and the table.**

1 Valentina Tereshkova _____ born in Russia on March 6, 1937.

2 The training program _____ very easy.

3 There _____ 400 people interested in going to space.

4 These moments _____ very important for her.

> **RULE:** *Was/Were* is the past form of _____ .

Affirmative	Negative
I/he/she/it ¹_____ we/you/they **were** there **was** / ²_____	I/he/she/it **wasn't (was not)** we/you/they ³_____ (**were not**) there ⁴_____ / **weren't**

2 **Complete the sentences with *was*, *wasn't*, *were*, or *weren't*.**

1 My friends and I ___*were*___ at the mall yesterday. My sister _____ there, too, but my parents _____ because they _____ at work.

2 There _____ lots of people at the beach yesterday. There _____ a little girl with her dog. The dog _____ very nice. Its name _____ Ollie.

Workbook page 90

VOCABULARY
Time expressions: past

1 🔊 2.31 **Write *in*, *at*, *last*, and *yesterday* to complete the time expressions. Listen and check.**

1 _____ weekend / Sunday / night / week / month / year

2 _____ morning / afternoon / evening

3 _____ 2014

4 _____ four o'clock / 5:30 / 6:00 a.m. / 6:30 p.m.

2 **Look at the pictures. Write sentences in your notebook to say where the people were and when. Use *in*, *at*, *last*, or *yesterday*.**

at the movies | in Paris | at the soccer game
at a birthday party | at the park | at her grandparents'
Lillian was at the park at a quarter after eleven yesterday morning.

3 **Make notes about where you were yesterday at the times in the pictures in Exercise 2. Where were you in July 2014?**

4 **SPEAKING Work in pairs. Tell your partner where you were yesterday. Find out about your partner.**

> *I was at home at a quarter after eleven, yesterday morning. What about you?*

> *I was at my cousin's house.*

5 **SPEAKING Use the information about your partner to report to the class.**

> *Yesterday morning, Maria was at home. At half past three yesterday afternoon, she was at a friend's house. In the evening, she was at the movies with her mom.*

A Lillian
B Joseph
C Leo
D Sam
E Camilla
F Evelyn

Workbook page 93

LISTENING

1 Look at the picture. Where was Ethan on Saturday evening? Where was Tamara? Use ideas from the box to help you.

> On Saturday evening, Ethan was …
> There were …
> He was …
> The … were happy because …
>
> Tamara was …
> The band was …
> The music was …
> There were … / She was …

2 ▶ 2.32 Listen to the dialogue and check your answers.

3 ▶ 2.32 Listen again and match the questions with the answers.

0	Does Ethan say it was a good party?	e
1	Were there a lot of people?	
2	Who were the five special guests at the party?	
3	What was the name of the band?	
4	Were the people in R5 at the party?	
5	How was the music for Ethan?	

a No, there weren't.

b R5.

c It wasn't bad.

d They were from a band.

e Yes, he says it was fantastic.

f No, they weren't, but their music was.

GRAMMAR
Simple past: be (questions)

1 In your notebook, put the words in the correct order to make questions.

1 you / the movies / were / at / ?

_____

2 the music / good / was / ?

_____

3 many / guests / were / there / ?

_____

2 Match the answers below with the questions in Exercise 1. Then complete the table.

	a	Yes, it was.		b	No, there weren't.
	c	No, I wasn't.			

Question	Short answer
Was I/he/she/it …? 1_____ we/you/ they …?	Yes, I/he/she **was**. No, I/he/she 2_____. Yes, we/you/they 3_____. No, we/you/they **weren't**.

3 ▶ 2.33 Complete the dialogue with *was, were, wasn't,* or *weren't.* Then listen and check.

JEN   Oh no!

PEDRO   What's wrong?

JEN   My phone! Where is it? It 0 __was__ in my jacket!

PEDRO   OK, calm down. Where 1_____ your phone this morning?

JEN   Well, I 2_____ at home from nine to ten o'clock.

PEDRO   And then? 3_____ you downtown?

JEN   Yes, I 4_____ . I 5_____ at the mall. And I'm 100% certain that my phone 6_____ in my pocket.

PEDRO   7_____ Steve and Marta with you?

JEN   No, they 8_____ . I 9_____ alone.

PEDRO   OK. At the mall, which stores 10_____ you in?

JEN   Only the shoe store.

PEDRO   Wait a minute. Let me call you.

JEN   It's ringing! Oh, look, in the shoe bag! It 11_____ there all the time!

Workbook page 90 ▶

FUNCTIONS
Asking for information about the past

1 Write *was* or *were* to complete the questions. Then ask and answer the questions with a partner. Check your answers on page 93.

1 _____ Valentina Tereshkova born in Russia?

2 _____ her parents astronauts, too?

3 _____ there 400 people interested in the competition?

4 _____ the flight very easy or very difficult?

5 _____ the Olympic games in Russia in 2013?

2 Make notes to answer the questions.

1 Where were you at 3:00 on Saturday?

2 What was your hobby when you were eight?

3 How old were you in May 2014?

4 How old was your best friend last year?

3 SPEAKING Work in pairs. Ask and answer the questions in Exercise 2.

READING

1 Look at the photos of two movie heroes. What do you know about them? What special powers do they have?

2 **◀))2.34** Read and listen to the article and check your answers.

Fictional heroes

Who is she? Storm

What's her story?

Storm's story started in New York, where she was born. Her mom was a princess and her dad worked as a photographer. When Storm was six, she moved to Cairo, Egypt, with her parents. One day a plane crashed into their house. Storm's parents died, and she was alone in the big city. Her life in Cairo was very hard. When she was a teenager, Storm discovered that she had special powers, and she started to use them – not always successfully.

What are her powers?

Storm has control over the weather. She can change the temperature. She can make rain, sunshine, hurricanes, clouds, and storms.

Who is he? Percy Jackson

What's his story?

His father was Poseidon, the Greek god of the sea. His half-brother was named Tyson. Tyson was a monster. At first, Percy hated his monster brother. Later, Percy and Tyson tried to help each other in their many adventures. In the end, they were friends. Percy was never afraid, and he never worried about his life. He helped the people he liked.

What are his powers?

Percy is very strong because he is the son of the god of the sea. He's a very fast swimmer. He can stay underwater for a long time. He can talk to sea animals, and he can make sea storms.

3 Read the article again. Mark the sentences T (true) or F (false).

0	Storm was born in a city in the U.S.	T
1	Storm's parents died in a city in the U.S.	☐
2	Storm's family moved to Egypt.	☐
3	Storm was good at using her special powers at the beginning.	☐
4	Percy's father was the god of hurricanes.	☐
5	Percy and Tyson were not friends at the beginning.	☐
6	Percy's brother was a monster.	☐

▮ TRAIN TO THiNK ▮

Sequencing

1 Put the sentences in order to tell Kidhero's story.

☐	a	There was a very fast car on the street.
8	b	Kidhero was very happy.
☐	c	There were also two young children in the street.
1	d	It was a hot day, and Kidhero wanted an ice cream.
☐	e	He walked to an ice cream shop.
☐	f	Kidhero jumped in front of the car and stopped it with his hand.
☐	g	He saved the children.
☐	h	He walked out of the shop with his ice cream.

2 **SPEAKING** Work in pairs. Tell the story. Can you include these lines?

He walked back home.

Kidhero started to run.

The children smiled.

GRAMMAR
Simple past: regular verbs

1 Write the base forms of the verbs.

Base form	0 *help*	1	2	3
Simple past	helped	started	moved	tried

2 Complete the sentences from the stories on page 96 with the past forms from Exercise 1. Then complete the rule.

1 Storm's story _____ in New York.
2 When Storm was six, she _____ to Cairo.
3 Percy and Tyson _____ to help each other.
4 He _____ the people he liked.

> **RULE:** To form the simple past of regular verbs, add
> ¹_____ to the base form.
> When the verb ends in -*e*, just add -*d*.
> When the verb ends in consonant + -*y*, change *y* to
> ²_____ and add -*ed*.

3 Write the simple past forms of these verbs. Check your answers in the text on page 96.

0 work   *worked*   3 crash _____
1 die _____   4 like _____
2 hate _____   5 worry _____

4 Complete the text about Bruce Wayne. Use the simple past form of the verbs in parentheses.

SUPER heroes

Bruce Wayne is Batman. When Bruce Wayne was a child, he and his parents were in the streets of Gotham City and a man ⁰___*attacked*___ (attack) them. The man ¹_____ (kill) Bruce's parents. The police ²_____ (arrive) too late. After this, Bruce ³_____ (decide) to fight crime.

For many years, Bruce ⁴_____ (train) hard to become a crime fighter. He ⁵_____ (call) himself "Batman," and ⁶_____ (try) hard to fight the bad people in Gotham. His best friend was James Gordon, a police officer. He had other friends, too. They all ⁷_____ (help) him to fight the criminals of Gotham.

Workbook page 91

Pronunciation
Simple past: regular verbs
Go to page 121.

VOCABULARY
The weather

1 🔊 2.37 Match the sentences in the list with the pictures. Write 1–8 in the boxes. Listen and check.

1 ~~It's raining.~~ | 2 It's sunny. | 3 It's windy.
4 It's cloudy. | 5 It's snowing. | 6 It's hot.
7 It's cold. | 8 It's warm.

A

B

C

D

E

F

G   1

H

2 Complete the dialogues with some of the phrases from Exercise 1. Sometimes there is more than one correct answer.

0 A What's the weather like?
   B ___*It's raining*___ , so take an umbrella.
1 A Bye, Mom.
   B Bye. But you don't need a sweater. _____ outside.
2 A Hey look! _____ !
   B Great! We can go skiing later!
3 A Wow, _____ today.
   B I know! You need to hold on to your hat!

3 **SPEAKING** Work in pairs. Write similar dialogues and act them out.

Workbook page 93

Culture

Statues

There are many strange and wonderful statues all over the world.

Charles La Trobe was an important man in Melbourne, Australia, in the 1800s. He improved the city for people. For example, he created a lot of parks. These days in Melbourne there are lots of things to remember him by. There's a La Trobe University and a La Trobe Street. There's a statue of him at the University. It's upside down!

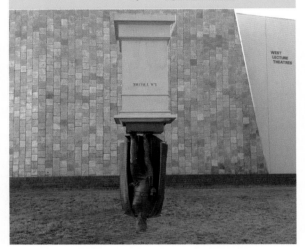

Franz Kafka was a writer from Prague, Czech Republic. He was born in 1883. His books were in German. During his life he was not very famous, but now he is. Many of his stories were very strange. There's a very unusual statue of him in Prague. He's sitting on the shoulders of an empty suit!

Hidesaburō Ueno was a professor at Tokyo University. Every day he traveled to work by train. When he arrived home in the evening, his dog Hachiko always waited at the station for him. One day Mr. Ueno died. He never arrived home again. For eight more years Hachiko waited at the station every day. When Hachiko died, they made a statue of him. You can see it at the station.

In the middle of the Atacama Desert in Chile, a big hand comes out of the sand. It's 70 kilometers from the nearest town. *Mano de Desierto* (The Hand of the Desert) is 11 meters tall. It's the work of the Chilean sculptor Mario Irarrázabal.

1 Look at the photos on page 98. Where are these things in the photos?

desert | sand | shoulders
suit | upside down

2 ◀)2.38 Read and listen to the article. Where are the statues?

3 Read the article again. Mark the sentences T (true) or F (false).

0 Charles La Trobe helped the people of Melbourne. | T
1 Franz Kafka was from Germany.
2 Kafka's stories were unusual.
3 Hachiko loved his owner, Mr. Ueno, very much.
4 Mr. Ueno's dog waited to meet him at home every day.
5 "The Hand of the Desert" is the hand of a famous Chilean sculptor.

WRITING
A statue in my town

1 Read what Maggie, from Manchester, wrote. Who does she want a statue of and why?

2 Read the text again. Find and <u>underline</u> examples of *was* / *were* and other verbs in the simple past.

3 Which parts of the text talk about these things? Write a, b, or c in the boxes.

a = why the band should have a statue
b = where the writer is from and who the statue is of
c = what the band did

4 Imagine you can choose to have a statue of a famous person (or famous people) in your city. Make notes about these things.

1 Where you live.
2 Who the person is / people are.
3 What the person/people did.
4 Why you think there should be a statue.

5 Write a short text with the title "A Statue in My Town."

1 Use Maggie's text to help you.
2 Use your ideas from Exercise 4.
3 Write about 50 words.
4 Check that you used the simple past tense correctly.

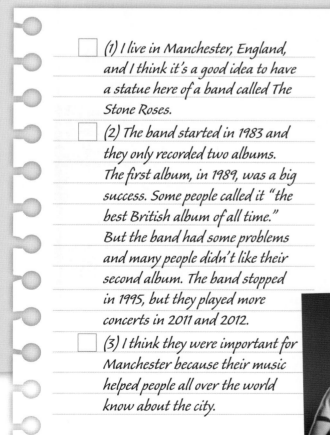

☐ *(1) I live in Manchester, England, and I think it's a good idea to have a statue here of a band called The Stone Roses.*

☐ *(2) The band started in 1983 and they only recorded two albums. The first album, in 1989, was a big success. Some people called it "the best British album of all time." But the band had some problems and many people didn't like their second album. The band stopped in 1995, but they played more concerts in 2011 and 2012.*

☐ *(3) I think they were important for Manchester because their music helped people all over the world know about the city.*

READING AND WRITING
Part 3: Dialogue matching

1 Complete the conversation between Marco and a waiter. What does Marco say to the waiter?

For questions 1–5, choose the correct letter A–H.

WAITER	Can I help you?
MARCO	(0) ___E___
WAITER	Of course, here you are.

(a few minutes later)

WAITER	Are you ready to order?
MARCO	(1) _____
WAITER	Very good. And what would you like to drink?
MARCO	(2) _____
WAITER	Would you like a dessert?
MARCO	(3) _____
WAITER	Certainly.

(45 minutes later)

WAITER	How was your meal?
MARCO	(4) _____
WAITER	Can I get you anything else?
MARCO	(5) _____
WAITER	Of course.

A Yes, please. Can I have the apple pie?
B No, just the check, please.
C How much is the pasta?
D It was great, thank you.
E Yes, can I have the menu, please?
F Yes, I am. Can I have the pizza, please?
G Where's the restroom?
H An orange juice, please.

Part 9: Guided writing

2 Read the email from your friend Luca.

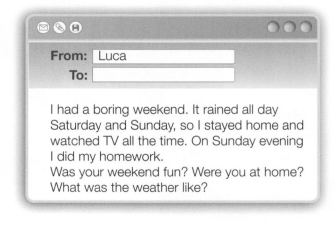

From: Luca
To:

I had a boring weekend. It rained all day Saturday and Sunday, so I stayed home and watched TV all the time. On Sunday evening I did my homework.
Was your weekend fun? Were you at home? What was the weather like?

From:
To:

Write an email to Luca and answer the questions. Write 25–35 words.

VOCABULARY

1 **Complete the sentences with the words in the list. There are two extra words.**

at | carrots | cloudy | in | juice | last | meat
oranges | raining | sandwich | warm | yesterday

1 It's a beautiful day today. It's _____ and sunny.
2 School started again _____ morning.
3 I love vegetables. _____ are my favorite.
4 He was born _____ 1994.
5 She arrived _____ half past three.
6 Would you like a chicken _____ or a hamburger?
7 It's very _____ today. I hope the sun comes out later.
8 There was a lot of rain _____ night.
9 Do you want something to drink? Some _____ , maybe?
10 No chicken or lamb, please. I don't eat _____ .

/10

GRAMMAR

2 **Complete the sentences with the words in the list.**

can | must | must not | was | were | would

1 _____ you like eggs for breakfast?
2 It _____ a very windy day yesterday.
3 It's her birthday tomorrow. We _____ remember to say "Happy Birthday."
4 _____ we watch TV now, please?
5 Meet me at the train station at six o'clock. You _____ be late!
6 There _____ 200 people at the game on Saturday.

3 **Find and correct the mistake in each sentence.**

1 Yesterday we play computer games at home.   _____
2 There was five bananas here. Where are they now?   _____
3 I must to do some work tonight.   _____
4 Can I having a green salad, please?   _____
5 I tried to call you yesterday, but there was no answer. _____
6 I'm thirsty. I like some milk, please.   _____

/12

FUNCTIONAL LANGUAGE

4 **Complete the missing words.**

1 A Do you want some h _ _ _ with your homework?
   B No, t _ _ _ _ _ _ , I'm OK.
2 A Where were you y _ _ _ _ _ _ _ _ _ afternoon?
   B I w _ _ at home. Why?
3 A Can you o _ _ _ the window, please?
   B Yes, of c _ _ _ _ _ _ .
4 B C _ _ I use your phone, please?
   B Sure, no p _ _ _ _ _ _ _ .

/8

MY SCORE [ ] /30

| 22 – 30 |
| 10 – 21 |
| 0 – 9 |

11 | A WORLD OF ANIMALS

OBJECTIVES

FUNCTIONS: talking about past vacations; talking about ability in the past; describing a photo; sequencing (in a story)

GRAMMAR: simple past: irregular verbs; simple past (negative and questions); *could / couldn't*

VOCABULARY: verb collocations; adjectives

READING

1 Match the words in the list with the photos. Write 1–12 in the boxes.

1 bear | 2 bird | 3 cat | 4 cow | 5 dog
6 elephant | 7 gorilla | 8 horse | 9 tiger
10 rabbit | 11 sheep | 12 snake

2 Complete the sentences with (plural) animals. Then compare your ideas with other students. Use the animals from Exercise 1 or others that you know.

0 Sometimes _____*snakes*_____ are dangerous.

1 Sometimes you see _____ in people's houses.

2 You can find _____ in towns.

3 You can find _____ in the countryside.

4 I like _____ .

5 I don't like _____ .

6 You can find _____ on a farm.

7 _____ can sometimes run very fast.

8 You can find _____ in Africa.

9 People sometimes eat _____ .

3 🔊 2.39 Look at the photos on page 103. What do you think the article is about? Then read, listen, and check.

4 Read the article again. Choose the correct words.

0 Erin *worked* / *was on vacation* in Glacier Park.

1 The people wanted to *see bears* / *go horseback riding*.

2 Erin and the boy were on *the same horse* / *different horses*.

3 The boy's horse was so scared that it *ran away* / *couldn't move*.

4 *Tonk* / *Erin* didn't want to move.

5 The boy *fell off* / *didn't fall off* the horse.

6 *Erin* / *Erin and Tonk* ran at the bear three times.

7 *Erin saved the boy* / *The boy saved Erin* from the bear.

Erin and Tonk to the rescue

Erin Bolster and Tonk

Erin Bolster was a guide in Glacier Park in Montana, U.S. In July 2011, she took a group of eight people horseback riding in the woods. Erin was on a big white horse named Tonk.

Everyone was ready to have fun, and the ride started well. Erin knew there were bears in the woods, but they didn't usually go near people.

Suddenly, an angry, 300-kilogram grizzly bear came out from the trees. The bear was very near an eight-year-old boy who was on his horse. The boy's horse saw the bear and got very scared. It ran away with the boy on its back. The bear ran after them.

Tonk was scared, too. He didn't want to move, but Erin needed to help the boy. She didn't stop to think. She gave Tonk a kick, and they went after the bear.

She found the bear near the boy and his horse. Then the boy fell off the horse, and the bear started to go toward him! Erin put Tonk between the bear and the boy. Together they ran at the bear three times. The bear made a terrible noise, but then it went away. Erin picked the boy up and took him back to his father and the other riders.

The boy's father was very happy, and Erin and Tonk were heroes!

▇ THiNK VALUES ▇

Animals and us

1 After Erin and Tonk saved the boy, Erin decided to buy Tonk. Why? Choose an answer.

   A Tonk didn't have a place to live.
   B Erin thought Tonk was a hero.
   C Tonk was very cheap.
   D Erin thought Tonk was a beautiful horse.

2 Check (✓) the things you agree with.

   ☐ It's important to be kind to animals.
   ☐ Animals and people can live together.
   ☐ It isn't good to eat animals.
   ☐ It isn't good to use animals for clothes.
   ☐ All animals are important.
   ☐ Zoos are bad for animals.
   ☐ Zoos help people understand animals.
   ☐ It isn't good to have animals in your house.

3 **SPEAKING** Work in pairs. Compare your ideas with a partner.

GRAMMAR
Simple past: irregular verbs

1 **Look at these examples from the article on page 103. Find the past tense of the other verbs in the article and write them in the table.**

Erin **put** Tonk between the bear and the boy. Together they **ran** at the bear three times.

0 run	*ran*	6 give	
1 put		7 go	
2 come		8 know	
3 fall		9 make	
4 find		10 see	
5 get		11 take	

2 **Complete the sentences with the simple past form of the words in the list. Use the irregular verbs list on page 128 of the Workbook to help you.**

come | drink | eat | fall | forget | get
give | go | run | see | take | write

1 Last weekend we __went__ to New Mexico. My uncle _____ with us.
2 We _____ some nice places and _____ lots of photos.
3 The little girl _____ too fast, and she _____ down.
4 I _____ some good gifts for my last birthday. My parents _____ me a bicycle!
5 I _____ an email to my friend, but I _____ to send it!
6 My friends and I had a huge dinner last night. We each _____ a pizza and _____ two milkshakes!

Simple past: negative

3 **These sentences are not true. Use the article on page 103 to correct them. Complete the rule.**

0 Bears usually went near people.
  Bears didn't usually go near people.
1 Tonk wanted to move.
  _____
2 Erin stopped to think.
  _____

> **RULE:** To make negative sentences in the simple past, we use *didn't* (*did not*) + the [1]*base / past* form of the verb.
> It's [2]*the same / different* for regular and irregular verbs.
> It's [3]*the same / different* for all subjects (I/you/they/we/he/she/it).

4 **Make the verbs negative.**

0 I went to the movie.	*didn't go*
1 I saw my friend at the party.	_____
2 We had a good time.	_____
3 I took a picture with my phone.	_____
4 Our friends came to see us.	_____
5 She found her phone.	_____

Workbook page 100

VOCABULARY
Verb collocations

1 **Choose the correct words in the sentences from the article on page 103.**

1 Everyone was ready to *have / do* fun.
2 The bear *did / made* a terrible noise.
3 The boy's horse *got / did* very scared.

2 **Write the phrases in the correct columns. You can write some phrases in more than one column.**

a break | a good time | a mistake | a noise
a shower | angry | away | excited | homework
on vacation | photos

have	take	make
	a break	
do	get	go

3 **Add the words in the list to the correct column(s) in Exercise 2. Can you think of more words to add?**

a bath | a party | a train | breakfast | fun | skiing

4 **Complete the sentences so they are true for you. Use an affirmative or negative form of the verb.**

1 I _____ breakfast this morning.
2 I _____ my homework last night.
3 Last weekend, I _____ a lot of pictures at the party.
4 I _____ a good time at the park.
5 My family _____ on vacation last year.
6 The last time I went to a party, I really _____ fun.

5 **SPEAKING** Compare your answers with a partner.

Workbook page 103

LISTENING

1 🔊 **2.40** **It's the end of the summer. Jack meets Bella and asks about her vacation. Listen and choose the correct options.**

1 Where did Bella go?

2 Where did Bella stay?

3 What did Bella see on her vacation?

2 🔊 **2.40** **Listen again and choose the correct answers.**

1 Where did Bella's dad work in the past?
  A in Belize   **B** in a zoo   **C** in a store for animals

2 What animals did Bella's family want to see?
  A snakes   **B** birds   **C** big cats

3 What did they hear outside the tent?
  A jaguars   **B** Bella's dad   **C** other people

■ THiNK SELF-ESTEEM ■
Animals and nature

Check (✓) the statements that are true for you.

- [ ] I like camping.
- [ ] It's exciting to be near animals and nature.
- [ ] I only want to see animals in a zoo.
- [ ] I don't like dangerous animals or places.

GRAMMAR
Simple past (questions)

1 **Complete the questions from the listening. Write the same word in each space. Then complete the rule.**

1 _____ you have a good vacation?

2 _____ you see any exciting animals?

3 Where _____ you stay, then?

4 What _____ you do on your vacation?

> **RULE:** To form simple past questions, we use _____ + I/you/he/she/it/we/they + the base form of the verb.

2 **Put the words in order to make questions.**

0 to the party / Did / go / you / ?
  Did you go to the party?

1 she / a good time / Did / have / ?
  _____

2 watch / on TV / Did / that show / you / ?
  _____

3 they / a lot of / take / photos / Did / ?
  _____

4 What / for breakfast / did / have / you / ?
  _____

5 did / you / Where / last night / go / ?
  _____

3 **Complete the mini-dialogues.**

0 **A** What *did you watch* on TV last night?
  B I watched a really good movie.

1 **A** Where _____ on Saturday?
  B I went to the movies.

2 **A** What _____ at the zoo?
  B We saw some really cool animals!

3 **A** What _____ in Mexico?
  B We ate tacos and salad.

4 **SPEAKING** **Work in pairs. Write questions to ask your partner about their last vacation. Then ask and answer.**

... go?   ... stay?   ... do?   ... a good time?   ... photos?   ... on your own?

Workbook page 101 ➤

Pronunciation
Simple past: irregular verbs
Go to page 121.

READING

1   Look at the pictures. These animals don't exist today; they are extinct. Match them with the names in the article. Write 1–3 in the boxes.

2   ◀》2.43 Read and listen to the article. Where did these animals live?

A

Extinct animals

1 The dodo

The dodo was a bird. It lived on the island of Mauritius, in the Indian Ocean. At one time there were thousands of them on the island. Then people from Europe arrived and started to eat them. The Europeans also brought animals such as dogs and cats with them to the island, and those animals ate the dodo's eggs. So, why didn't the dodo fly away from the people? Because it couldn't fly. And in 1681, the dodo became extinct.

2 Saber-toothed cats

These dangerous animals lived thousands of years ago in North and South America. They had two very big teeth. You could see these teeth even when the cat's mouth was closed. People think that these cats could kill very big animals with their long teeth. Saber-toothed cats became extinct around 10,000 BCE because there wasn't enough food for them.

B

3 The woolly rhinoceros

This very big animal lived in the middle of Europe and Asia until about 8,000 BCE. It had two horns – the big one was sometimes one meter long. It had a thick woolly coat, so it could keep warm in the cold winters. When the weather changed, the woolly rhinoceros couldn't live in the warm weather. Also, many people killed these animals for food. So the woolly rhinoceros slowly died out.

3   Read the article again. Write the names.

0   This kind of animal became extinct when the weather changed.
     woolly rhinoceros

1   These animals became extinct because of people.
     _____ _____

2   This kind of animal killed other animals.
     _____

3   This kind of animal was a bird, but couldn't fly.
     _____

4   This kind of animal was the first to become extinct.
     _____

5   This kind of animal was the last to become extinct.
     _____

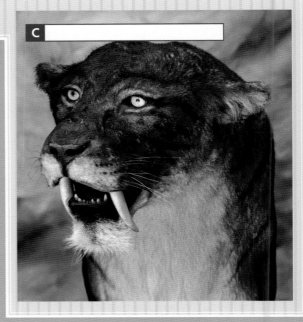

C

GRAMMAR
could / couldn't

1 **Complete the examples from the article on page 106. Then read the rule.**

1 These cats _____ kill very big animals.

2 The woolly rhinoceros _____ live in the warm weather.

> **RULE:** We use *could / couldn't* + the base form of a verb to talk about ability in the past.

2 **Use *could / couldn't* and a verb from the list to complete the sentences.**

~~do~~ | drive | play | ride | see | speak

0 The homework last night was very difficult. I
   ___*couldn't do*___ it! ✗

1 My grandma _____ well, so she got new glasses. ✗

2 My brother _____ the guitar when he was only seven. ✓

3 I _____ a bicycle when I was four. ✓

4 My father _____ a car until he was 25. ✗

5 My grandfather was amazing; he _____ five languages. ✓

3 **SPEAKING** Work in pairs. Think about what you could or couldn't do when you were five. Use the ideas in the list. Add your own ideas.

read and write
ride a bicycle
speak English
swim
use a tablet
dance
play the piano

> When I was five, I couldn't ride a bicycle.

> When I was five, I could swim.

> When I was five, I could play the piano.

Workbook page 101 →

VOCABULARY
Adjectives

1 🔊2.44 **Write a word from the list under each picture. There are six extra words you don't need. Listen and check.**

beautiful | boring | clean | dangerous | ~~dirty~~
interesting | mean | nice | safe | smart | stupid | ugly

0 ___*dirty*___

1 _____

2 _____

3 _____

4 _____

5 _____

2 **Match the adjectives and their opposites from Exercise 1.**

___*dirty*___ – ___*clean*___

_____ – _____

_____ – _____

_____ – _____

_____ – _____

_____ – _____

3 **SPEAKING** Work in pairs or in small groups. Use the adjectives from Exercise 1 to talk about these things.

your town | a TV show
a famous person | an animal
a sport that is popular in your country
a famous actor | a place in your country

Workbook page 103 →

The spider

1 **Look at the photos and answer the questions.**

1 What do you think Ruby is afraid of?
2 Is Dan nice or mean to Ruby?

2 🔊 2.45 **Now read and listen to the photostory. Check your answers.**

1

TOM I had a really good time yesterday.
DAN Yeah? What did you do?
TOM I took the dog for a walk in the forest. It was really fun.
ELLIE That sounds nice.

2

ELLIE What about you, Ruby? What did you do yesterday?
TOM Ruby? What's wrong? Did something bad happen?
RUBY Yes. Oh, it was terrible. I don't want to talk about it.
TOM Come on, Ruby. We're your friends. What happened?

3

RUBY Well, last night I went into my bedroom, and suddenly, I saw ... oh, it's stupid.
ELLIE What, Ruby? What? Tell us!
RUBY All right. I sat down on my bed, and there was a spider, right beside me! A big, fat, ugly spider.
ELLIE Oh, you poor thing!
DAN Ha, ha, ha! You're afraid of spiders? I don't believe it!
ELLIE Dan! Don't be so mean! Don't say things like that.
RUBY I hate spiders, Dan! I'm really, really afraid of them!

4

TOM That wasn't very nice, Dan. Tell her you're sorry.
DAN Oh, come on. It's silly to be scared of spiders.
TOM But she's really angry with you now.
DAN I have a great idea, Tom! Let's play a joke on her.
TOM Oh, no! Don't look at me!

DEVELOPING SPEAKING

3 ◼◄ **EP6** Watch to find out how the story continues.

1 What does Dan do?

2 What does Jason have?

4 ◼◄ **EP6** Watch again. Put the events in order. Write 1–7 in the boxes.

☐	a	Ruby tells Ellie about the trick.
☐	b	Ellie talks to a boy named Jason.
☐	c	Jason and Ellie meet with Dan at school.
☐	d	Tom says he's scared of Ellie.
☐	e	Dan gets scared when he sees Jason's pet.
1	f	Dan plays a trick on Ruby with a plastic spider.
☐	g	Dan tells Ruby that he understands how she feels.

PHRASES FOR FLUENCY

1 Find the expressions 1–4 in the story. Who says them?

1 What happened? _____

2 … suddenly … _____

3 All right. _____

4 You poor thing! _____

2 How do you say the expressions in Exercise 1 in your language?

3 Put the sentences in the correct order to make a dialogue.

☐	ANDY	I was in the kitchen, and, suddenly, I fell off my chair.
☐	ANDY	Yes! I was so scared I jumped onto the chair and then fell off.
☐	ANDY	I saw a big, scary spider!
1	ANDY	Can I tell you what happened yesterday?
☐	GINA	What? You saw a spider and fell off your chair?
☐	GINA	All right. What happened?
☐	GINA	Oh, you poor thing! But why did you fall?

4 Complete the mini-dialogues with the expressions from Exercise 1.

0 A You look really happy! _What happened?_

   B I got my test results. 95%!

1 A I think I'm sick.

   B _____ ! Maybe you should stay in bed today.

2 A Julia was so mean last night.

   B I know! At first she was OK – but _____ she started shouting at everyone!

3 A There's a great new online computer game. Can I play it, Dad?

   B _____ , but only for ten minutes. You have homework to do.

FUNCTIONS
Sequencing (in a story)

1 Read the blog entry. The writer is an animal. Choose which animal the writer is.

a bird   b cow   c cat

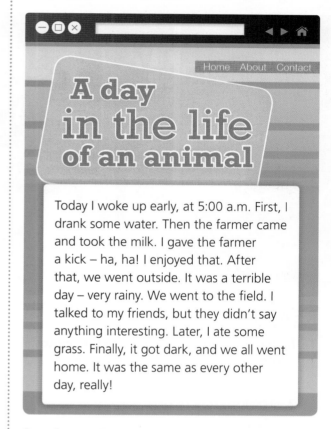

Home About Contact

A day in the life of an animal

Today I woke up early, at 5:00 a.m. First, I drank some water. Then the farmer came and took the milk. I gave the farmer a kick – ha, ha! I enjoyed that. After that, we went outside. It was a terrible day – very rainy. We went to the field. I talked to my friends, but they didn't say anything interesting. Later, I ate some grass. Finally, it got dark, and we all went home. It was the same as every other day, really!

2 Choose the words and phrases that say when things happened and the order in which they happened.

WRITING
A day in the life of an animal

1 Choose an animal. Choose from the animals on page 102 or think of a different one.

Think about:

- what this animal usually does every day
- what the animal eats and drinks
- where the animal goes

2 Write a blog entry for the animal. Don't write what animal it is! Use the simple past and sequencing words and phrases. Write 35–50 words.

3 Give your blog entry to a partner. Can he/she guess which animal it is?

12 | GETTING AROUND

OBJECTIVES

FUNCTIONS: talking about travel and transportation; comparing things; at the train station

GRAMMAR: comparative adjectives; *one / ones*

VOCABULARY: transportation; geographical places

A

B **1**

C

D

E

READING

1 Match the words in the list with the photos. Write 1–5 in the boxes under the photos.

1	a bike		3	a bus		5	a subway train	
2	a boat		4	a car				

2 **SPEAKING** Work in pairs. When do you use the types of transportation in Exercise 1?

> *I go to my friend's house by bike.*

> *I go to school by bus.*

3 Put the types of transportation in Exercise 1 in order of speed: 1 = slow, 5 = fast.

4 **◄))2.46** Read and listen to the article and write the type of transportation under the medal they would win.

1 _____

2 _____

3 _____

4 _____

5 Read the article again and match the questions with the answers.

0	Why did the TV show hosts have a race?	*d*
1	Why did they choose different types of transportation?	
2	Why was the result a surprise?	
3	Why were the hosts unhappy?	
4	What did the hosts say about the bike?	
5	Why is the bike a good form of transportation in a city?	

a   To find the best one.

b   Because the car didn't win.

c   Because it is a cheap, clean, and healthy form of transportation.

d   To find the best way to get across Manhattan.

e   It was dangerous.

f   Because the bike won.

A lot of big cities, like New York, have many traffic problems. Sometimes a trip of a few kilometers can take more than an hour. So what's the best way to get across Manhattan? For a very short trip, it's probably a good idea to walk. But what happens when you want to go farther?

The hosts of a popular TV car show decided to find out. Each of the hosts chose a different type of transportation to make the same trip. One host went by bike. One went by car. Another chose public transportation – the subway and the bus – and the last one traveled by speedboat up the Hudson River. They all started at the same time and the same place in Battery Park, but who got to Central Park first?

The results were a surprise. The bike came in first. In second place was the speedboat. Public transportation came in third, and the car was last.

So the hosts had an answer. The bike was quicker than all the other types of transportation, and the car was slower. They weren't very happy with the result because they wanted the car to win. They made a joke and said the bike wasn't a real winner because it was more dangerous.

But, of course, the bike is the real winner. It's the best way to get around. It's cheaper than public transportation and healthier for you than a car. It's also better for our cities because bikes don't pollute the air. So next time you need to go into town, think before you and your parents get into the car. Ask yourselves, "Can we make this trip by bike?"

■ THiNK VALUES ■

Transportation and the environment

1 **Choose the title that best sums up the article.**

a Cars are great ☐

b The great race ☐

c Get on your bike ☐

d Be careful on your bike ☐

2 **How friendly to the environment are these types of transportation? Write 1–6 in the boxes: 1 = best, 6 = worst.**

☐ bus
☐ bike
☐ car
☐ motorcycle
☐ plane
☐ train

3 **SPEAKING** **Work in pairs. Compare your answers with a partner.**

> I think number 1 is a bike.

> I don't. I think number 1 is a train.

VOCABULARY
Transportation

1 🔊 2.47 **Match the words in the list with the photos. Write 1–6 in the boxes. Listen and check.**

1 ferry boat | **2** helicopter | **3** motorcycle
4 plane | **5** taxi | **6** train

A **1**

B

C

D

E

F

2 **Look at the photos in Exercise 1 and answer the questions.**

Which types of transportation travel …

1 on roads?   2 on rails?

3 on water?   4 in the air?

3 **SPEAKING** **Can you add any other types of transportation to the lists?**

Workbook page 111

GRAMMAR
Comparative adjectives

1 **Look at the article on page 111. Check the sentence that isn't true.**

1 Bikes are *cheaper than* public transportation.

2 Bikes are *healthier* for you *than* cars.

3 Cars are *more dangerous than* bikes.

4 Bikes are *better than* other types of transportation.

2 **Complete the table. Use the examples in Exercise 1 to help you. Then complete the rule.**

adjective	comparative	
cheap	1 _____	
big	bigger	
easy	easier	
healthy	2 _____	than
expensive	more expensive	
dangerous	3 _____	
good	4 _____	
bad	worse	

RULE:

- Short adjectives: We usually add *-er*.
  If the adjective ends in consonant + *-y*, change the *y* to ¹_____ , e.g. *easy – easier*.
  If the adjective ends in vowel + consonant, double the consonant (e.g. *big – bi**gger***).

- Long adjectives: Add the word ²_____ before the adjective.

- Irregular adjectives: Use a different word, e.g. *good – better, far –* ³_____ .

After comparative adjectives we use *than*.

3 **In your notebook, write the comparative form of these adjectives.**

1 exciting   3 difficult   5 safe   7 hot
2 slow   4 happy   6 funny   8 fast

4 **Look at the types of transportation on this page. Write four sentences to compare them.**
Planes are quicker than ferries.

5 **SPEAKING** **Work in pairs. Read your sentences to your partner, but don't say one of the types of transportation. Your partner guesses what it is.**

They are quicker than buses.   *Cars!*

Workbook page 108

Pronunciation
Word stress: comparatives
Go to page 121. 🔊

LISTENING

1 **◀))2.50** Amy wants to travel to New York City from Cold Spring. She's at the train station. Listen to the dialogue and complete the details of her trip.

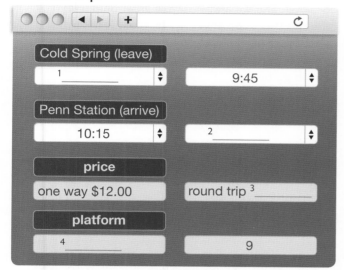

Cold Spring (leave)
| 1 _____ | 9:45 |

Penn Station (arrive)
| 10:15 | 2 _____ |

price
| one way $12.00 | round trip 3 _____ |

platform
| 4 _____ | 9 |

2 **◀))2.50** Listen again and answer the questions.

1 Why doesn't Amy want to take the 9:40 train to New York?
2 When does Amy want to return to Cold Spring?
3 Where is platform 13?
4 Who wants to meet Amy in New York?

FUNCTIONS
At the train station

1 Look at these sentences. Who says them? Write S (salesperson) or C (customer) in the boxes.

0	How can I help you?	S
1	What time's the next train to Cold Spring?	
2	What time does the 11:30 arrive in New York?	
3	How much is a ticket to New York?	
4	Do you want one way or round trip?	
5	That's $16.40, please.	
6	What platform does the train leave from?	
7	Have a great trip.	

2 **SPEAKING** Work in pairs. Use this information and prepare a similar dialogue. Act out your dialogue.

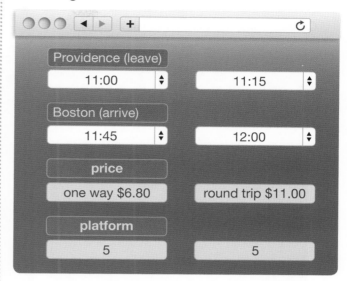

Providence (leave)
| 11:00 | 11:15 |

Boston (arrive)
| 11:45 | 12:00 |

price
| one way $6.80 | round trip $11.00 |

platform
| 5 | 5 |

■TRAIN TO THiNK■
Comparing

1 Write the words in the list in the correct place in the diagram.

cheap | dangerous | drive | engine | healthy
lights | quick | radio | ride | wheels

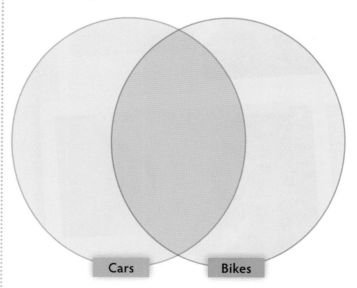

Cars   Bikes

2 Think of more words to add to the diagram.

3 **SPEAKING** Work in pairs. Compare the two forms of transportation. Use comparative adjectives.

> *In my city, bikes are quicker than cars.*

READING

1 🔊 2.51 **Read and listen to the magazine article. Write the names under the photos.**

Carlos | Miriam | Julia | Nathan

My **favorite** trip

A _____

B _____

C _____

D _____

Carlos

Every year my family goes on vacation to a small town by the ocean. It has really beautiful beaches, and we always have a great time. I love the trip there. We always go by train. It takes about four hours, but I don't mind. I'm always so excited. I just love watching the mountains and forests go by.

Julia

What's my favorite trip? Any one with my mom on her motorcycle. I don't care where we go, I just love being on her bike. She's a really good rider and I always feel safe. I love the wind on my face as we ride through the countryside.

Miriam

My favorite trip is my walk to school. We live on a farm, and my school is about one kilometer away. Every morning I walk across the fields and then I go along the river until I'm at my school in the village. It's a really beautiful walk and it's so quiet. I love my walk to school ... but I love the walk home more!

Nathan

My grandparents live in Miami. We visit them every year and, of course, we go by plane. It's a three-hour trip, but I love it. I love traveling by plane. It's so exciting. I never get bored because there are lots of movies to watch. They always have really good ones.

2 **Read the article again. Correct the information in these sentences.**

0 Carlos's family always go to ~~a different~~ place on vacation.
   the same _____

1 Carlos's train trip takes six hours.
   _____

2 Julia loves riding on the back of her dad's motorcycle.
   _____

3 Miriam likes her walk to the local store.
   _____

4 She likes the walk to school more than the walk home.
   _____

5 Nathan's aunt lives in Miami.
   _____

GRAMMAR
one / ones

1 Look at the examples from the article on page 114. What do the words *one* and *ones* refer to? Then complete the rule with *plural* and *singular*.

1 What's my favorite trip? Any **one** with my mom on her motorcycle!

2 I never get bored because there are lots of movies to watch. They always have really good **ones**.

> **RULE:** To avoid repeating a noun, we often use **one** in place of ¹_____ nouns and **ones** in place of ²_____ nouns.

2 Write *one* or *ones* in the spaces to replace the crossed out words.

0 **A** Do you want to watch this movie?
  B No, I've seen that ~~movie~~ ___*one*___ before.

1 **A** Do you want to try on these jeans?
  B No, I'd like to try on the ~~jeans~~ _____ over there.

2 **A** What bus can we take?
  B Any ~~bus~~ _____ that has "Boston" on the front of it.

3 I have three children. The oldest ~~child~~ _____ is a boy and the other ~~children~~ _____ are girls.

4 There's a bank on Main Street and another ~~bank~~ _____ on Castle Street.

5 I have lots of books, but my favorite ~~books~~ _____ are my bird books.

Workbook page 109

VOCABULARY
Geographical places

1 Complete the words with the first and last letters. Use the article on page 114 to help you.

2 SPEAKING Work in pairs.

Make a list of famous …
a beaches.
b rivers.
c oceans and seas.
d lakes.

3 Think about your favorite trip. Make notes.

Where to	
How	
Who with	

4 SPEAKING Tell your partner about your trip.

> My favorite trip is to the mountains to ski.

> Who do you go with?

> I go there with my family.

> How do you travel?

> We go by car.

Workbook page 111

0 *m* ountai *n*

1 __ eac __

2 __ ive __

3 __ cea __

4 __ iel __

5 __ ak __

6 __ ar __

7 __ ores __

Culture

Transportation
around the world

1 _____

2 _____

3 _____

4 _____

The bamboo train, Cambodia

This simple train is made from pieces of bamboo. Local people use it to travel and move things from one village to another. It has an engine on it and wheels from old trains. It uses the same rails as the national trains, and it's a quick way to travel. But be careful: when you hear a train coming, get out of the way fast!

The zorb, New Zealand

The zorb is not really a type of transportation, but it is a fun way of getting around. The zorb is a big plastic ball. One person gets inside and the zorb then rolls down the hill. There's a cushion of air to protect the person. It's an exciting way of getting down a hill, but it isn't so good for getting back up again!

The tuktuk, India

Tuktuks are originally from Thailand, but they are popular in many Asian countries. They have three wheels and an engine. The noise the engine makes gives the tuktuk its name. They are big enough for two people and a suitcase, and they are often used for making short trips across busy cities. They're small so they can go through the crowded streets quickly. The trip is often a little dangerous but always exciting.

The totora boat, Peru

Lake Titicaca is a large lake between Peru and Bolivia. The Uro people live in floating villages on the water. They use a local reed called totora to build their homes and boats. The totora boats are light but very strong. The Uro people build the boats to look like dragons to protect them and their homes.

1 **Look at the photos on page 116. Find these words. Which ones can you see in the photos?**

hill | a suitcase | an engine | bamboo | reed | (something that is) floating

2 🔊2.52 **Read and listen to the article and write the name of the transportation under the pictures.**

3 **Read the article again and check (✓) the boxes.**

	bamboo train	tuktuk	zorb	totora boat
1 It has an engine.	☐	☐	☐	☐
2 It has wheels.	☐	☐	☐	☐
3 It travels on water.	☐	☐	☐	☐
4 It can be dangerous.	☐	☐	☐	☐
5 It's exciting.	☐	☐	☐	☐

4 **SPEAKING** **Work in pairs. Discuss the questions.**

1 Which of these types of transportation would you most like to travel on?

2 Are there any unusual types of transportation in your country? Where?

WRITING
Unusual forms of transportation

1 **Read the article. What's the name of the vehicle?**

2 **Read the article again and answer the questions.**

1 What type of transportation is it?

2 Where is it?

3 Why is it unusual?

4 Who uses it?

3 **Choose one of these unusual types of transportation or one you already know about. Look on the Internet for information. Make notes to answer the questions in Exercise 2.**

The Katoomba Funicular, Australia

The Ice Angel, Wisconsin

The Chiva Express, Ecuador

4 **Use your notes to write a short description about that form of transportation. Write 35–50 words.**

Amsterdam

Amsterdam is the capital city of the Netherlands. It's a popular city for tourists and it's often pretty crowded in the summer months. It also has a lot of canals, so getting around by bus or car is often difficult. *The Flying Dutchman* is a new way of getting around the city. It's an amphibious bus. That means that it's a bus that can go on the roads but it can also travel on the water like a boat. At the moment, *The Flying Dutchman* offers short tours of the city for passengers waiting at the International airport.

READING AND WRITING
Part 7: Open cloze

1 **Complete the message left on a vacation blog. Write ONE word for each space.**

Every year my family goes **(0)** __*on*__ vacation to a small town by the sea. My grandparents live there. It **(1)** _____ really beautiful beaches. My favorite one is just next **(2)** _____ their house. I love the trip there. We always go **(3)** _____ train. It's quicker **(4)** _____ the car. It takes about three hours, but I don't **(5)** _____ . I **(6)** _____ always so excited. I just love watching **(7)** _____ mountains and forests go by. I take lots **(8)** _____ photos from the train window. I also play games **(9)** _____ my brother and my parents. We always **(10)** _____ a lot of fun.

LISTENING
Part 3: Three-option multiple choice

2 **⏴⏵2.53 Listen to Penny talking to her friend Seth about their pets. For each question, choose the right answer (A, B, or C).**

0 Spot is

A Penny's dog.　　　　B Seth's dog.　　　　C Seth's grandma's dog.

1 Floppy is a

A rabbit.　　　　B cat.　　　　C dog.

2 Penny's pet is a

A rabbit called Nemo.　　　　B fish called Nemo.　　　　C cat called Nemo.

3 Nemo eats once a

A day.　　　　B week.　　　　C month.

VOCABULARY

1 **Complete the sentences with the words in the list. There are two extra words.**

did | do | farm | forest | fun | get | go
had | mean | bike | safe | taxi

1 She isn't nice to me. I don't like _____ people.
2 Let's have some _____ this weekend. How about going to the mountains?
3 We went to Orlando last weekend, and we _____ a really good time.
4 There are lots of animals on that _____ .
5 It's snowing! Let's _____ skiing this afternoon.
6 Dangerous? No, it's completely _____ , I promise.
7 Sunday was really boring. I just _____ my homework and nothing else.
8 I don't think it's a good idea to ride a _____ on city streets.
9 It isn't really important. Please don't _____ mad about it.
10 We missed the train, so we took a _____ to get home.

/10

GRAMMAR

2 **Complete the sentences with the words in the list.**

better | couldn't | did | good | more | ones | went

1 I was sick, so I _____ go to your party. Sorry.
2 Blue? No, thanks, I like the red _____ over there.
3 I love this song. It's really _____ .
4 _____ you have fun last weekend?
5 My new phone was _____ expensive than my old one.
6 This movie is _____ than her last one.
7 My friends _____ to the concert, but I couldn't go with them.

3 **Find and correct the mistake in each sentence.**

1 Are these your new shoes, or are they the old one? _____
2 My parents gave me this book for my birthday. _____
3 The chicken was horrible, so I not ate it. _____
4 Went you to the movie theater last weekend? _____
5 This shirt is cheaper then the other one. _____
6 I'm bad at French, but Jack is more bad! _____
7 Did you saw any good movies last week? _____

/14

FUNCTIONAL LANGUAGE

4 **Complete the words.**

1 **A** Hi. Can I have a t _ _ _ _ _ to Ottawa, please?
  B OK. O _ _ w _ _ or r _ _ _ _ _ t _ _ _?
2 **A** What time is the n _ _ _ _ train to Philadelphia, please?
  B 3:00 – and after that, there's a train at 3:45.
  A OK. I want the 3:00 train. What platform does it l _ _ _ _ _ from?
  B Platform 4. Have a good t _ _ _!

/6

MY SCORE **/30**

| 22 – 30 |
| 10 – 21 |
| 0 – 9 |

PRONUNCIATION

UNIT 7
The /ɔ/ vowel sound

1 🔊2.03 **Read and listen to the dialogue.**

PAULA	What do you want to do this afternoon?
BRIAN	I'd like to play **ball**. There are **always** games in the park.
PAULA	OK, but it's **awfully** hot.
BRIAN	Of course it's hot, Paula! It's **August**!
PAULA	That's true. OK, a **ball** game sounds **awesome**!
BRIAN	Great. I just have to **call** my mom and tell her where we are.

2 Say the words in **blue**. Which vowel sound do they all have?

3 🔊2.04 Listen again and repeat. Then practice with a partner.

UNIT 8
Intonation: listing items

1 🔊2.17 **Read and listen to the dialogue.**

MOM	I'm going shopping. Do you want anything?
BRAD	Yes! I need a T-shirt. Oh, and some socks, please.
MOM	OK. A T-shirt and socks …
BRAD	Actually, I need a T-shirt, socks, sneakers, a jacket, and a baseball cap.
MOM	A T-shirt, socks, sneakers, a jacket, and a baseball cap. I think you need to come with me!

2 Brad wants *a T-shirt*, *socks*, *sneakers*, *a jacket*, and *a baseball cap*. Circle the arrows to show when his voice goes up and when it goes down.

3 🔊2.18 Listen again and repeat. Then practice with a partner.

UNIT 9
Intonation: giving two choices

1 🔊2.26 **Read and listen to the dialogue.**

WAITRESS	Would you like soup or salad?
MIKE	Salad, please.
WAITRESS	Chicken or fish?
MIKE	I think I'll have fish today.
WAITRESS	Would you like dessert?
MIKE	Yes, please!
WAITRESS	Cake or fruit?
MIKE	Hmm … I'll have fruit.
WAITRESS	And coffee or juice?
MIKE	Oh, coffee, please.

2 🔊2.26 Circle the arrows in the dialogue to show when the waitress' voice goes up and when it goes down. Listen and check.

3 🔊2.27 Listen again and repeat. Then practice with a partner.

UNIT 10
Simple past: regular verbs

1 🔊2.35 **Read and listen to the story.**

My grandmother **lived** in the country. She **walked** to town to go to school. She **finished** school when she was twelve. She **started** working in a bottle factory. She **worked** in the factory until she **married** my grandfather. One day, she **invented** a machine that cleaned bottles. The factory **wanted** the machine, and my grandparents were rich after that!

2 The -*ed* ending is pronounced differently in the blue, green, and red words. What's the difference?

3 🔊2.36 Listen again and repeat. Then practice with a partner.

UNIT 11
Simple past: irregular verbs

1 🔊2.41 **Read and listen to the dialogue.**

PAM	Where did you go last summer?
JOHN	I **went** to Kenya, in Africa.
PAM	What did you see?
JOHN	We **saw** lions, elephants, and zebras.
PAM	Who did you go with?
JOHN	I **went** with my parents.
PAM	Did you have a good time?
JOHN	We **had** a great time!

2 Say the past tense words in **blue**. Find the infinitive forms of the verbs in the dialogue.

3 🔊2.42 Listen again and repeat. Then practice with a partner.

UNIT 12
Word stress: comparatives

1 🔊2.48 **Read and listen to the sentences.**
A plane is faster than a car.
A bike is slower than a train.
A speedboat is quicker than a ferry.
A bike is easier to ride than a horse.

2 Find the comparative adjective in each sentence. Which syllable is stressed in each of these words?

3 🔊2.49 Listen again and repeat. Then practice with a partner.

GET IT RIGHT!

UNIT 7
can / can't

Learners sometimes use the wrong form of the verb when they use *can* and infinitive.

We use the base form of the verb after *can*.

✓ *He can play the piano.*
✗ *He* ~~can to play~~ *the piano.*

We use the infinitive after *want* and *need*.

✓ *They want to know the answer.*
✗ *They* ~~want know~~ *the answer.*

Correct the mistakes in the sentences.

0   He needs do that.
    He needs to do that.
1   Can you to speak Spanish?
2   We want do some shopping.
3   You need clean your room.
4   I need eat something. I'm hungry!
5   He can't does his homework.
6   Alex wants do everything.

UNIT 8
like / don't like + -ing

Learners sometimes use the wrong form of the verb where *-ing* is required.

We use the *-ing* form of verbs after the verbs *like*, *don't like*, *love*, and *hate*.

✓ *I like playing tennis.*
✗ *I* ~~like play~~ *tennis.*
✗ *I* ~~like to playing~~ *tennis.*

Correct the mistakes in the sentences.

0   I like read books.
    I like reading books.
1   I like sing and dancing.
2   We love go to the beach.
3   She hates watch baseball games.
4   They don't like play basketball.
5   Pedro doesn't hate study.
6   Anna likes to wearing white clothes.

UNIT 9
Modal verbs: spelling

Learners often have problems spelling modal verbs.

Correct the spelling mistakes in the sentences.

0   Wold you like to go with me?
    Would you like to go with me?
1   I cant find my book.
2   You mustnot stay out too late.
3   I woud like to play baseball.
4   You ca'nt use YouTube.
5   Mus you be so loud?
6   We cannt be late.

UNIT 10
Simple past: *be*

Learners sometimes confuse *was* and *were*.

***Was*, *wasn't*, *were*, and *weren't* all have to agree with the subject.**

✓ *The jeans were very beautiful.*
✗ *The jeans* ~~was~~ *very beautiful.*

Check (✓) the correct sentences and put an ✗ next to the incorrect ones. Correct the mistakes.

0	There was a lot of people.	✗
	There were a lot of people.	
1	We was at Dan's house all night.	
2	There was a lot of food.	
3	Wasn't you there?	
4	I were happy to see you on the weekend.	
5	How many people were at your house?	
6	Last night there were a party on the beach.	
7	He was my friend at school.	
8	Katie and Jo was there.	

UNIT 11
Simple past: irregular verbs

> **Learners sometimes use the wrong forms of irregular verbs in the simple past or misspell them.**
>
> ✓ *I paid a lot of money.*
> ✗ *I ~~payed~~ a lot of money.*

Correct the mistakes in the sentences.

0   I haved a good time.
   I had a good time.
1   I maked a lot of friends.
2   She gived me a lot of gifts.
3   Jack and Al taked photos.
4   There where some problems with his work.
5   I cam home late yesterday.
6   He swimmed very fast.
7   They goed to the movies.
8   Helen mad some food.

Simple past: negative

> **Learners sometimes use the simple present negative when the simple past is required.**
>
> ✓ *I didn't find the answer before the end of the exam.*
> ✗ *I ~~don't~~ find the answer before the end of the exam.*

Choose the correct words.

0   We *don't* / (*didn't*) go to the game last week.
1   I *didn't* / *don't* need any help at the moment.
2   I bought some T-shirts, but I *didn't* / *don't* buy any shoes.
3   I went to a cell phone store, but I *didn't* / *don't* like the phones there.
4   Do you like chicken? No, I *didn't* / *don't* eat meat.
5   I got a lot of gifts, but he *didn't* / *don't* give me one.
6   We *didn't* / *don't* usually go on vacation because we like being at home.

UNIT 12
Comparative adjectives

> **Learners often use *more* and the *-er* form of an adjective in the same sentence when only one of these is required.**
>
> **We form comparative adjectives by adding *-er* if the adjective has one syllable (or two syllables ending in *-y*), and by using *more* if the adjective has two or more syllables. We don't use *more* and *-er* together.**
>
> ✓ *This one is bigger than that one.*
> ✗ *This one is ~~more bigger~~ than that one.*
> ✗ *This one is ~~more big~~ than that one.*

Correct the mistakes in the sentences.

0   The train is more cheap than the plane.
   The train is cheaper than the plane.
1   He is more healthier than he was last year.
2   Enrique is more older than his brother.
3   I have the more newer cell phone.
4   Basketball is more good than baseball.
5   I was more happy than Joe at the end of the game.
6   Enrique's brother is more friendlier than Enrique.
7   The bus is more easy for me.

then, that, and *than*

> **Learners sometimes use *then* or *that* when *than* is required with comparative adjectives.**
>
> ✓ *Carlos is older than Juan.*
> ✗ *Carlos is older ~~then~~ Juan.*
> ✗ *Carlos is older ~~that~~ Juan.*

Complete the sentences with *then*, *that*, or *than*.

0   He can run faster ___*than*___ me.
1   It is much better _____ your cell phone.
2   Call me _____ .
3   It costs more _____ I thought.
4   _____ is my book.
5   This one is better than _____ one.
6   We ate dinner and _____ watched a movie.

STUDENT A

UNIT 8, PAGE 79, TRAIN TO THINK

Student A

Listen to the questions your partner asks about the picture in Exercise 1. Answer with short answers. Correct the negative answers.

1 Are there ten people in the band?
2 Is the singer wearing a red dress?
3 Are there two guitar players in the band?
4 Are there five trumpet players in the band?
5 Are all the band members wearing hats?

STUDENT B

UNIT 8, PAGE 79,
TRAIN TO THINK

Student B

Listen to the questions your partner asks about the picture in Exercise 1. Answer with short answers. Correct the negative answers.

1 Are there eight people dancing?
2 Are the two dancing women wearing green dresses?
3 Is one dancing man wearing a blue shirt?
4 Are eight people drinking?
5 Are four people sitting down?

This page is intentionally left blank.

Acknowledgments

The authors and publishers acknowledge the following sources of copyright material and are grateful for the permissions granted. While every effort has been made, it has not always been possible to identify the sources of all the material used, or to trace all copyright holders. If any omissions are brought to our notice, we will be happy to include the appropriate acknowledgments on reprinting.

The publishers are grateful to the following for permission to reproduce copyright photographs and material:

T = Top, B = Below, L = Left, R = Right, C = Center, B/G = Background p.66 (TL): © David Madison/CORBIS; p.66 (TR): © DPK-Photo / Alamy; p.66 (TC): versh / Shutterstock; p.66 (TC): Tim Hawley / Getty Images; p.67 (TL): Dave Nenna/ The Firecrackers; p.67 (TR): courtesy of The Bolton News; p.67 (CL): Konstantin Chernichkin (UKRAINE) / Reuters; p.67 (CL): Jeff R. Bottari / Getty Images; p.68 (BL): Paul Bradbury / Shutterstock; p.68 (BL): Fotosearch / Getty Images; p.68 (BC): Andy Crawford / Getty Images; p.68 (BR): © PCN Photography / Alamy; p.68 (BL): © H. Mark Weidman Photography / Alamy; p.68 (BC): © Lev Dolgachov / Alamy; p.68 (BR): © Olga Rozenbajgier/moodboard/Corbis; p.68 (BL): Mike Kemp / Getty Images; p.69 (TL): © RTimages / Alamy; p.69 (TL): Dmitry Zimin / Shutterstock; p.69 (BR): © Michael Burrell / Alamy; p.70 (TC): ©KIKE DEL OLMO/AP/PA Images; p.70 (BR): ©KIKE DEL OLMO/AP/ PA Images; p.71 (TL): © RTimages / Alamy; p.71 (TL): © caia image / Alamy; p.71 (TL): © StockbrokerXtra / Alamy; p.71 (TL): © Cris Kelly / Alamy; p.74 (TL): Patrik Giardino / Getty Images; p.74 (TC): © Johner Images / Alamy; p.74 (TR): © Danita Delimont / Alamy; p.74 (CL): Don Bayley / Getty Images; p.74 (CR): © Thomas Photography LLC / Alamy; p.75 (TL): Richard Johnson / www. richard-johnson.co.uk/; p.75 (TR): Richard Johnson / www.richard-johnson. co.uk/; p.77 (TL): © Robert Harding World Imagery / Alamy; p.77 (TL): Bruce Yuanyue Bi / Getty Images; p.77 (TL): © Jane Tregelles / Alamy; p.77 (TL): Izzet Keribar / Getty Images; p.80 (TL): © Gergely Zsolnai / Alamy; p.80 (CL): Lynn Gai / Getty Images; p.80 (CR): © dbimages / Alamy; p.81 (BL): Hero Images / Getty Images; p.81 (BR): Caiaimage/Martin Barraud / Getty Images; p.84 (TL): Sam Edwards / Getty Images; p.84 (TL): Crazy World / Shutterstock; p.84 (TC): Marzia Giacobbe / Shutterstock; p.84 (TR): B. and E. Dudzinscy / Shutterstock; p.84 (C): ElenaGaak / Shutterstock; p.84 (CR): Scruggelgreen / Shutterstock; p.85 (TR): Arina P Habich / Shutterstock; p.85 (CL): Arina P Habich / Shutterstock; p.85 (CR): siamionau pavel / Shutterstock; p.86 (TR): Floortje / Getty Images; p.86 (TR): Creativ Studio Heinemann / Getty Images; p.86 (TR): © age fotostock / Alamy; p.86 (TR): © Lilyana Vynogradova / Alamy; p.86 (TR): © Danny Smythe / Alamy; p.86 (TR): © Jon Helgason / Alamy; p.86 (TR): © D. Hurst / Alamy; p.86 (TR): © Vitaliy Pakhnyushchyy / Alamy; p.86 (TR): © Feng Yu / Alamy; p.86 (TR): © Andrzej Tokarski / Alamy; p.86 (TR): © JOHN KELLERMAN / Alamy; p.86 (TR): © Feng Yu / Alamy; p.86 (TR): © Feng Yu / Alamy; p.86 (TR): asajdler / Getty Images; p.86 (TR): © Judith Collins / Alamy; p.86 (TR): © Feng Yu / Alamy; p.88 (TL): Tom Grill / Corbis; p.92 (TL): © Thomas Imo / Alamy; p.92 (TC): Erik Simonsen / Getty Images; p.92 (C): © Image Source Plus / Alamy; p.92 (CL): © 2happy / Alamy; p.92 (TR): © NASA / Alamy; p.92 (CR): © Andrew Paterson / Alamy; p.92 (BL): © Tim Graham / Alamy; p.92 (BL): © Chuck Nacke / Alamy; p.93 (TL): © RIA Novosti / Alamy; p.93 (TR): © ITAR-TASS Photo Agency / Alamy; p.96 (TR): © Photos 12 / Alamy; p.96 (BR): © Photos 12 / Alamy; p.98 (TL): Brian King / OnlyMelbourne; p.98 (TR): © Igor Stevanovic / Alamy; p.98 (BL): © MIXA / Alamy; p.98 (BR): © Kseniya Ragozina / Alamy; p.88 (BR): Mike Prior/Redferns / Getty Images; p.88 (BR): Samir Hussein/Getty Images; p.100 (MR): FredFroese / Getty Images; p.102 (TL): © Radius Images / Alamy; p.102 (TL): © Oleg Kozyrev / Alamy; p.102 (TR): © Radius Images / Alamy; p.102 (TR): © Johner Images / Alamy; p.102 (TL): © Design Pics Inc / Alamy; p.102 (TL): © Design Pics Inc / Alamy; p.102 (TL): Martin Willis / Getty Images; p.102 (TL): © Westend61 GmbH / Alamy; p.102 (TR): Design Pics/John Short / Getty Images; p.102 (TR): © Radius Images / Alamy; p.102 (TL): Johner Images / Alamy; p.102 (TL): Westend61 / Getty Images; p.103 (TL): Erin Bolster; p.103 (CR): © Gunter Marx / Alamy; p.106 (TR): © Stocktrek Images, Inc. / Alamy; p.106 (TC): © Stocktrek Images, Inc. / Alamy; p.106 (BC): © Arterra Picture Library / Alamy; p.110 (TL): © Rob Crandall / Alamy; p.110 (CR): Bruce Yuanyue Bi / Getty Images; p.110 (CR): © Eric Bechtold / Alamy; p.110 (TR): Jodie Wallis / Getty Images; p.110 (TL): Panhandlin / Getty Images; p.112 (TL): Steven Miric / Getty Images; p.112 (TL): Olaf Loose / Getty Images; p.112 (TL): Meinzahn / Getty Images; p.112 (TL): P_Wei / Getty Images; p.112 (TL): © Design Pics Inc / Alamy; p.112 (TL): © Nando Machado / Alamy; p.112 (BL): © Konrad Bąk / Alamy; p.112 (BL): © Radius Images / Alamy; p.112 (BL): © Stephen Dorey ABIPP / Alamy; p.112 (BL): © Andrew Paterson / Alamy; p.113 (TR): © Sean Pavone / Alamy; p.114 (TR): Alinute Silzeviciute / Shutterstock; p.114 (TR): D.R. Hutchinson / Getty Images; p.114 (CR): Onzeg / Getty Images; p.114 (CR): Stefano Oppo / Getty Images; p.116 (TL): © Peter Titmuss / Alamy; p.116 (TL): kevinjeon00 / Getty Images; p.116 (TR): © Rafael Ben-Ari / Alamy; p.116 (TL): © eran yardeni / Alamy; p.116 (TR): © Michele Burgess / Alamy; p.117 (B): Paulo Amorim / Getty Images; p.118 (C): © MELBA PHOTO AGENCY / Alamy; p.127 (TL): © Erik Reis / Alamy; p.127 (TL): alexey_ boldin / Getty Images; p.127 (TL): © Digifoto Green / Alamy; p.127 (TL): © Aydin Buyuktas / Alamy; p.127 (TL): © D. Hurst / Alamy; p.127 (TL): pictafolio / Getty Images; p.127 (BL): © Newscast-online Limited / Alamy; p.127 (BL): © Konstantin Gushcha / Alamy.

Commissioned photography by: Mike Stone p 72, 90, 108.

Cover photographs by: (L): ©Tim Gainey/Alamy Stock Photo; (R): ©Yuliya Koldovska/Shutterstock.

The publishers are grateful to the following illustrators:
Christos Skaltsas (hyphen) 77, 78, 79, 82, 87 (R), 91, 94, 95, 96, 97, 105, 107, 110, 115, 127, 128 and Zaharias Papadopoulos (hyphen) 76, 87 (L)

The publishers are grateful to the following contributors: Hyphen: editorial, design, and project management; CityVox, LLC: audio recordings; Silversun Media Group: video production; Karen Elliott: Pronunciation sections; Matt Norton: Get it Right! sections

AMERICAN ThiNK

WORKBOOK STARTER

A1

Herbert Puchta, Jeff Stranks & Peter Lewis-Jones

CAMBRIDGE
UNIVERSITY PRESS

This page is intentionally left blank.

CONTENTS

7 WE LOVE SPORTS!

GRAMMAR

can / can't for ability SB page 68

1 ★☆☆ Match the sentences with the pictures. Write 1–8 in the boxes.

 A ☐

 C ☐

 E ☐

 G ☐

B ☐

D ☐

 F ☐

 H ☐

1 He can ride a bike.
2 They can sing.
3 She can swim.
4 We can dance.
5 We can't dance.
6 She can't swim.
7 They can't sing.
8 He can't ride a bike.

2 ★★☆ Match the questions and answers.

0 Can you and Lucia sing? e
1 Can you speak Spanish? ☐
2 Can David play the piano? ☐
3 Can Elena cook? ☐
4 Can a race car go fast? ☐
5 Can Karim and Jamal ride a bike? ☐

a No, he can't.
b Yes, they can.
c Yes, I can.
d Yes, it can.
e No, we can't.
f Yes, she can.

3 ★★★ Write sentences with *can* or *can't*.

0 I / ride a bike (✓) / skateboard (✗)
   I can ride a bike, but I can't skateboard.

1 I / sing (✓) / dance (✗)
   _____

2 my little brother / talk (✗) / walk (✓)
   _____

3 they / speak Spanish (✓) / speak English (✗)
   _____

4 my dad / drive (✗) / cook (✓)
   _____

5 we / do somersaults (✗) / spin (✓)
   _____

6 my mom / play the piano (✗) / play the guitar (✓)
   _____

7 the bird / sing (✓) / talk (✗)
   _____

Pronunciation
The /ɔ/ vowel sound
Go to page 120.

4 ★★★ Look at the pictures and write questions with *can*. Then answer them so they are true for you.

0 *Can you drive?*

Yes, I can. / No, I can't.

1 _____

_____

2 _____

_____

3 _____

_____

4 _____

_____

5 ★★★ Complete the sentences with your own ideas.

1 I can't _____ , but I can

_____ .

2 My best friend can _____ ,

but she/he can't _____ .

3 My teacher can't _____ , but

she/he can _____ .

4 Babies can _____ , but they

can't _____ .

5 My mom can _____ , but she

can't _____ .

6 My dad can't _____ , but he

can _____ .

7 The cat can _____ , but it can't

_____ .

Prepositions of time `SB page 71`

6 ★☆☆ (Circle) the correct options.

0 I leave home *in / on / (at)* 7:00 a.m. to go to school.

1 Karina's birthday is *in / on / at* May.

2 The movie starts *in / on / at* 8:00 p.m.

3 It's very cold here *in / on / at* the winter.

4 I don't go to school *in / on / at* Sundays.

5 There's a holiday *in / on / at* November 23 this year.

6 We play volleyball *in / on / at* Friday afternoons.

7 The first day of school is *in / on / at* the 7th.

7 ★★☆ Complete the sentences with *at*, *in*, or *on*.

1 The party is __*on*__ Friday _____ 7:00 p.m.

2 School starts _____ 8:00 a.m. and it finishes _____ 3:00 p.m.

3 It's very hot _____ summer.

4 My school vacation starts _____ June and ends _____ September.

5 My birthday is _____ March 21. It's _____ the spring. This year it's _____ a Tuesday.

8 ★★☆ Write the words in the correct columns.

Friday | May | noon | midnight | seven o'clock
September | the evening | the morning
the fall | 3:30 p.m. | the 4th of July | May 22

in	on	at
May	Friday	3:30 p.m.

GET IT RIGHT!
Prepositions of time

We use *on* for days of the week and dates.

✓ I go swimming **on** Saturday.

✗ I go swimming ~~in~~ Saturday.

✗ Her birthday is ~~in~~ May 1.

We use *at* for clock times.

✓ My dance lesson is **at** five o'clock.

✗ My dance lesson is ~~on~~ five o'clock.

We use *in* for months and seasons.

✓ Is your birthday **in** October?

✗ Is your birthday ~~at~~ October?

✗ We often go to the beach ~~at~~ the summer.

Complete the sentences with *on*, *in*, or *at*.

0 I will be there __*on*__ Sunday evening.

1 He wants to go to your house _____ July 7.

2 I can come _____ Monday or Friday.

3 My final exams are _____ June.

4 Can you meet me _____ twelve thirty?

5 The trees are so pretty _____ the fall.

6 It starts _____ a quarter to ten.

VOCABULARY

Sports

- ice-skate
- play basketball
- cycle
- snowboard
- play volleyball
- play baseball
- do tae kwon do
- go surfing

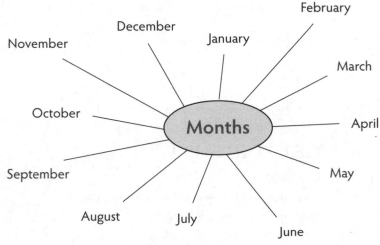

Months

- November
- December
- January
- February
- October
- March
- April
- September
- May
- August
- July
- June

Telling time

1 It's three o'clock.

2 It's eight thirty.

3 It's a quarter after ten.

4 It's a quarter to one.

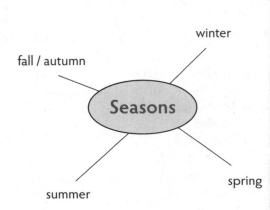

Seasons

- fall / autumn
- winter
- summer
- spring

Ordinal numbers

1st – first	5th – fifth	9th – ninth	13th – thirteenth
2nd – second	6th – sixth	10th – tenth	20th – twentieth
3rd – third	7th – seventh	11th – eleventh	30th – thirtieth
4th – fourth	8th – eighth	12th – twelfth	31st – thirty-first

Key words in context

final	The **final** game of the season is this Saturday.
hit	In table tennis you **hit** a ball with a paddle.
hobby	My **hobby** is soccer. I like watching it and playing it.
jump	My cat can **jump** very high.
jump rope	Lots of girls at our school like playing with **jump ropes**.
organize	Mr. Thomas **organizes** all the music and theater shows at our school.
somersault	I can't do a **somersault**. I'm not a gymnast!
spin	I like **spinning** in circles.
winner	The **winner** of the race gets $1,000.

Sports SB page 68

1 ★☆☆ Look at the pictures and write sentences.

 0 Liz

 1 Adam

 2 Dina

 3 Connor

 4 Ethan

 5 Dylan

 6 Chloe

7 Josh

0 *Liz ice skates.*

1 _____

2 _____

3 _____

4 _____

5 _____

6 _____

7 _____

Telling time SB page 69

2 ★★☆ Write the times under the clocks.

0

It's seven o'clock.

1

_____

2

_____

3

_____

4

_____

5

_____

Months and seasons SB page 71

3 ★★☆ Complete the months and seasons with the missing consonants.

Months

1 O _ _ o _ e _
2 _ u _ e
3 A _ _ i _
4 _ e _ e _ _ e _
5 _ a _
6 _ u _ _
7 _ a _ u a _ _
8 A u _ u _ _
9 _ e _ _ e _ _ e _
10 _ o _ e _ _ e _
11 _ e _ _ u a _ _
12 _ a _ _ _

Seasons

13 _ u _ _ e _
14 _ a _ _
15 _ _ _ i _ _
16 _ i _ _ e _

4 ★★★ Choose four months. Say what season they are in and what you do then.

0 *August is in the summer. I go on vacation with my family in August.*

1 _____

2 _____

3 _____

4 _____

Ordinal numbers SB page 71

5 ★☆☆ Complete the table.

1st	*first*		fifth	9th			thirteen
	second	6th		10th		20th	
3rd		7th			eleventh	30th	
4th		8th		12th			thirty-first

6 ★★☆ Write the ordinal numbers.

14th *fourteenth*   21st _____   27th _____   22nd _____

28th _____   15th _____   16th _____   23rd _____

29th _____   24th _____   17th _____   18th _____

19th _____   26th _____   25th _____

READING

1 **REMEMBER AND CHECK** Match each person with two facts. Then look at the article on page 67 of the Student's Book and check your answers.

1 Nikolai Kutsenko   [e]   [ ]
2 Xavier Good   [ ]   [ ]
3 Tillman   [ ]   [ ]
4 The Firecrackers   [ ]   [ ]

a enjoys golf.
b are gymnasts.
c is a dog.
d use music for the show.
e has a world record.
f is a little boy.
g is awesome with a soccer ball.
h can skateboard.

2 Read the text and complete the sentences under the pictures.

Sports for All

The Paralympic Games are a big sporting event for athletes with disabilities. The games take place every two years: after the Summer Olympics and after the Winter Olympics. They show the world all the amazing things that these sportspeople can do. Here are two awesome Paralympians.

This is [1]_____.
She's from [2]_____.

This is [3]_____.
He's from [4]_____.

Terezinha Guilhermina is from a poor family in Betim in Brazil. She can't see very well, but she can run. She can run very fast. She runs with the help of her guide, Guilherme Soares de Santana. Guilherme can run fast, too, but he can see. He helps Terezinha stay on the track. Terezinha is very successful. She is a Paralympian gold medal winner in the 200-meter race. She wants to win a gold medal in her home country at the Rio 2016 Olympics.

David Weir is a wheelchair athlete from the U.K. He has a problem with his legs. He can't use them to run or walk, so he races in a special wheelchair. He moves the wheelchair with his hands. He races any distance from 100 meters to a full marathon. He has six gold medals from the Paralympic Games in Beijing and London. He is also a six-time winner of the London Marathon. David is very popular with his fans. They call him the "Weirwolf."

3 Read the text again and answer the questions.

0 When do the Paralympic Games happen?   *Every two years.*
1 What can't Terezinha do? _____
2 Who helps Terezinha run? _____
3 What race does she have a gold medal from? _____
4 What can't David Weir do? _____
5 How does he move his wheelchair? _____
6 How many gold medals does he have from the Paralympic Games in Beijing and London? _____

DEVELOPING WRITING

An amazing person

My cousin Tom is an amazing person. He's from San Diego and he's the junior champion of California at tae kwon do. He's only 13, but he can pick his dad up and throw him on the couch. He has a black belt. Tom's also really good at school. He's really great at math and science and he can speak three foreign languages: Mandarin Chinese, Portuguese, and Spanish.
I like Tom because he's a really good friend to me. He's also really funny. He can always make me laugh.

My ⁰ *Grandmother Ana* is an amazing person. We live in the same city, ¹_____ , so I see her a lot. She's 72 years old and she still ²_____ every day. She's on a team, and she races most weekends. She swims in special races for people over 65. She always wins. She's really fast. She can ³_____ . She loves swimming. It makes her feel young. I like her because she's really ⁴_____ to me. And she ⁵_____ !

1 Read the text. Imagine you're the writer of the text and answer the questions.

0 Who is he?
My cousin Tom

1 Where is he from?
_____

2 What does he do?
_____

3 What sort of things can he do?
_____

4 Why do you like him?
_____

2 Read the answers to the questions and use them to complete the text.

1 Who is she?
Grandmother Ana

2 Where is she from?
Mexico City

3 What does she do?
swims

4 What sort of things can he/she do?
swim 400 meters in five minutes

5 Why do you like her?
friendly / bakes great cakes

3 Answer the questions about an amazing person you know.

1 Who is he/she?
_____

2 Where is he/she from?
_____

3 What does he/she do?
_____

4 What sorts of things can he/she do?
_____

5 Why do you like him/her?
_____

4 Use your answers to the questions in Exercise 3 to write a short text about that person. Write 35–50 words.

_____
_____
_____
_____
_____
_____

LISTENING

1 🔊 **31** Listen and match the dialogues with the pictures. Write 1–3 in the boxes.

A ☐

B ☐

C ☐

2 🔊 **31** Listen again and draw the times on the clocks.

Dialogue 1:
What time do they play tennis?

Dialogue 2:
Which movie time do they choose?

Dialogue 3:
What time do they decide to meet downtown?

3 🔊 **31** Listen again and complete each sentence with one word.

0 Laura feels a little _____*bored*_____ .

1 Laura is _____ until 1:00 p.m.

2 Trisha wants to go to the movies in the
   _____ .

3 The first movie is at six _____ .

4 Martina wants to go _____ with Dan.

5 Martina leaves _____ at five.

DIALOGUE

Put the dialogue in order.

☐ **BEN** We can't. I don't have a ball.

☐ **BEN** TV? That's why I'm bored. I'm tired of watching TV.

☐ **BEN** We can't. She's away on vacation.

[1] **BEN** I'm bored. What can we do?

☐ **SUE** Is she? So how about some more TV?

☐ **SUE** Why don't we play basketball?

☐ **SUE** No ball. OK, let's go to Jayne's house.

PHRASES FOR FLUENCY SB page 73

1 Match the questions with the answers.

0 Are these your pens and books? [c]

1 Oh, no. It's raining. ☐

2 I can't find my phone! ☐

3 Look, the bus just left. <u>Now what?</u> ☐

a <u>It's no big deal.</u> I have an umbrella.

b <u>I'm sure</u> it's in your backpack. Look again.

c No, I think that's Owen's <u>stuff.</u>

d Don't worry. There's another in 15 minutes.

2 Complete the dialogue with the words and phrases that are underlined in Exercise 1.

MOM Come on, Ted. It's time for school.

TED I'm ready, Mom.

MOM Do you have your swimming
0_____*stuff*_____ ?

TED I don't have swim practice today.

MOM 1_____ you do, Ted. It's Thursday.

TED It's Thursday? Oh, no. I have swim practice! But my towel's wet. 2_____?

MOM 3_____ . You can take a different towel.

TED Thanks, Mom. You're the best.

Sum it up

1 Read and write the names of the sports.

Welcome to a day of sports on BCB TV.

We have a great schedule of sporting action for you this Saturday.

☆ We have live ⚽ 0 _soccer_ from London, where Chelsea play Manchester United in the big game.

☆ We have 🏀 1 _____ – ALL the action from the NBA.

☆ There's 🏐 2 _____ action from last night's game between Brazil and Spain.

☆ There's live ⚾ 3 _____ from one of today's Super League matches.

☆ And we have ⛸ 4 _____ from Helsinki.

There's something for everyone.

2 Read the clues and complete the TV sports schedule.

Start time	End time	Sports program
_____ p.m.	_____ p.m.	_____
_____ p.m.	_____ p.m.	_____
_____ p.m.	_____ p.m.	_____
_____ p.m.	_____ p.m.	_____
_____ p.m.	_____ p.m.	_____

1 The afternoon of sports starts at 1:00 p.m.
2 Baseball is the fourth program.
3 The ice-skating is on for half an hour.
4 Soccer is after volleyball.
5 Basketball starts six hours after ice skating ends.
6 The soccer starts at 3:00 p.m.
7 Baseball is on for two and a half hours.
8 Volleyball is on for an hour and a half.
9 There are eight hours of sports.
10 Ice-skating is the first sport.
11 The last show is an hour and a half.

3 Put the words in the list into four categories. There are three words in each category. Name the categories.

August | cycling | fifth | first | June | May | snowboarding | spring | summer | tae kwon do | third | winter

1 MONTHS	2	3	4
August			

DANCE TO THE MUSIC

GRAMMAR
Present continuous `SB page 76`

1 ★ ☆ ☆ (Circle) the correct options.

0 She isn't here. She ('s)/ 're playing soccer in the park.

1 What *is / are* you doing?

2 Sorry, I can't talk now. I *'m / 's* watching a movie on TV.

3 All my friends are here. We *'s / 're* having a good time!

4 My brother's in his room. He *'s / 're* playing computer games.

5 My mom and dad *is / are* taking the dog for a walk.

6 I think they're happy. They *'s / 're* smiling a lot!

7 Look! There's Jimmy. Where *'s / 're* he going?

2 ★ ☆ ☆ Write the *-ing* form of these verbs.

0	shop	*shopping*	7	walk	_____
1	play	_____	8	read	_____
2	give	_____	9	take	_____
3	sit	_____	10	try	_____
4	dance	_____	11	stop	_____
5	smile	_____	12	write	_____
6	run	_____	13	draw	_____

3 ★★ ☆ Complete the sentences with the present continuous form of the verbs in parentheses.

0 Stop it, Jack. I ____*'m not talking*____ to you! (not talk)

1 Let's go for a walk. It _____. (not rain)

2 _____ you _____ the concert? (enjoy)

3 _____ your brother _____ a good time at college? (have)

4 What _____ you _____, Joaquim? (do)

5 The TV is on, but they _____ it. (not watch)

6 Maria! You _____ to me! (not listen)

7 What _____ the cat _____ ? (eat)

8 They _____ well today. (not play)

4 ★★ ☆ Mia is telling Ty about a new game show on TV. Complete the dialogue with the present continuous form of the verbs in parentheses.

MIA Well, there's a great new game show on TV. There are two teams. One player on a team 0 ____*is watching*____ (watch) a video on a tablet. Of course the other players can't see what 1_____ (happen) on the screen.

TY So?

MIA Well, the player with the tablet says things like, "A boy 2_____ (run). He 3_____ (wear) shorts. He 4_____ (hold) a ball." After each sentence the other players guess what 5_____ (happen) in the video.

TY And then what?

MIA The players can ask ten questions.

TY Like "What 6_____ they _____ (do) in the video?"

MIA No, of course not. They can only ask questions like "7_____ the boy _____ (play) with friends?" or "8_____ they _____ (go) to school?" or "9_____ they _____ (watch) a soccer game?"

TY And then?

MIA Sometimes the player watching the video says what 10_____ (not happen). Things like, "The boy 11_____ (not sitting) on the floor" or "The people 12_____ (not play) music." And the other player gets a point if they can say what's happening in the video.

TY Hmm. I don't like watching game shows. I like watching movies.

MIA Oh. Well, please watch tonight. There's a surprise for you!

TY A surprise? Really? Now I want to watch it!

5 ★★★ **Complete this extract from the game show with the correct form of the verbs in the list.**

hit | hold | kick | not go | not smile
not throw | play (x3) | stand | ~~wear~~

HOST OK! Let's play! Mia, you have the tablet, so your team starts.

MIA I can see twelve girls. They ⁰ _'re wearing_ shorts and T-shirts.

SIMON ¹_____ they _____ a game?

MIA Yes, they are. They ²_____ with a ball.

TOM ³_____ they _____ the ball with their feet?

MIA No, they aren't. And they ⁴_____ the ball. One girl ⁵_____ the ball in her hand. She ⁶_____ behind a line on the floor.

MARK ⁷_____ she _____ the ball with her hand?

MIA Yes, she is. But the ball ⁸_____ into the net. That's not good. She isn't happy. She ⁹_____ .

SIMON I know! ¹⁰_____ they _____ volleyball?

MIA Yes, they are!

HOST Good job! That's one point for you.

6 ★★★ **What do you think your family and friends are doing now? Look at the example and write similar sentences about them.**

0 _I think my sister is watching TV now._
1 _____
2 _____
3 _____
4 _____
5 _____

like / don't like + -ing [SB page 78]

7 ★★☆ **Write sentences with the correct form of the verbs.**

0 I / like / read / long books
I like reading long books.

1 my sister / not like / play / basketball
_____

2 my parents / hate / watch / science fiction movies
_____

3 my best friend / like / listen to / classical music
_____

4 I / not like / go to / the movies
_____

5 I / love / read / in bed
_____

8 ★★☆ **Complete the text. Use *love* (☺☺), *like* (☺), *don't/doesn't like* (☹), *hate* (☹☹), and the correct form of the verbs.**

My family is a little strange – they like or don't like all kinds of different things. My sister ⁰_ _doesn't like cooking_ _ (☹ cook), but she ¹_____ (☺☺ clean) her room. My father ²_____ (☹☹ go) for walks, but he ³_____ (☺☺ go) for a ride on his bike. My mother ⁴_____ (☺ read) magazines, but she ⁵_____ (☹☹ read) books. My parents ⁶_____ (☺ travel), but they ⁷_____ (☹ go) to other countries. And me? Well, I just ⁸_____ (☺☺ be) with my strange family!

9 ★★★ **Complete the sentences so they are true for you.**

0 I love _____ _singing in the shower_ _____ and _____ _going to the movies._ _____
1 I love _____
  and _____
2 I like _____
  and _____
3 I don't like _____
  and _____
4 I hate _____
  and _____

GET IT RIGHT! 👁
Present continuous

We use subject + *am/is/are* + -ing form of the main verb.

✓ *We are* watching TV.
✗ ~~We watching TV.~~
✓ *I am* eating a sandwich.
✗ ~~I am eat a sandwich.~~

Complete the sentences with the correct present continuous form of the verbs.

0 She _is taking_ (take) some photos of her cat.
1 We _____ (do) the laundry at the moment.
2 _____ (you / listen) to rap music?
3 He _____ (wear) a black shirt and jeans.
4 They _____ (walk) to the supermarket.
5 Who _____ (play) this video game?
6 He _____ (not eat) a sandwich, he's eating a burger!

VOCABULARY

Verbs

base form	-ing form
cheer	cheering
dance	dancing
leave	leaving
read	reading
run	running
sing	singing
sit	sitting
smile	smiling
stand	standing
take	taking
talk	talking
wear	wearing

Key words in context

concert	There's a **concert** tomorrow night and it's my favorite band!
deep	The water in the swimming pool is very **deep**. It's about three meters.
hold	Please **hold** my bag, so I can open the door.
instrument	The trumpet and the violin are musical **instruments**.
musician	He's a **musician**. He plays in a rock band.
relaxing	I love this gentle music. It's very **relaxing**.
singer	I think Taylor Swift is a very good **singer**.
size	What **size** shoes do you wear?
trumpet	My brother plays the **trumpet**.
violin	She's learning to play the **violin**.

Verbs SB page 76

1 ★☆☆ **Look at the picture above and complete the sentences with the correct form of the verbs in the list.**

cheer | dance | leave | read | ~~run~~ | sing
sit | smile | stand | take | talk | wear

0 Peter is _____*running*_____ .
1 Callie is _____ .
2 Charles is _____ .
3 Lucy is _____ on a bench.
4 Joe and Keri are _____ .
5 Jorge is _____ a hat.
6 Elena is _____ .
7 Rob is _____ .
8 Claire is _____ on her phone.
9 Matt is _____ a photo.
10 Gabriela is _____ .
11 Jess and David are _____ the park now.

2 ★★☆ **Complete each sentence with a verb from Exercise 1. Use the correct form of the verbs.**

0 I'm _____*reading*_____ a really good magazine. It's very interesting!
1 My dad's crazy. He wants to _____ a marathon.
2 Let's _____ a song.
3 This train _____ at 10:45, and arrives in Washington at 12:40.
4 Look at Mike! He's _____ green pants and a pink shirt!
5 _____ a photo of me, please.
6 I love _____ on the phone with my friends.
7 This is my favorite chair. I love _____ here.

Clothes SB page 79

3 ★☆☆ **Find twelve pieces of clothing in the word search.**

T	R	O	U	D	E	D	J	A	N	S	T
A	S	H	I	R	T	R	A	S	E	H	P
S	A	T	H	L	O	E	W	K	S	I	R
T	R	E	A	I	N	S	X	C	R	R	E
S	N	A	E	J	O	S	H	O	E	S	T
H	T	L	O	T	S	A	U	S	S	W	A
E	R	B	K	R	H	B	N	Y	T	E	E
R	I	R	W	E	O	U	K	J	N	A	W
L	H	A	D	I	R	Y	L	U	A	F	S
P	S	C	O	A	T	T	R	N	P	E	A
J	T	R	I	K	S	G	E	S	A	R	M
U	M	B	E	S	N	E	A	K	E	R	S

4 ★★☆ **Circle the odd one out in each list.**

0 (jeans)   sweater   shirt
1 socks   sneakers   coat
2 shorts   T-shirt   pants
3 dress   skirt   shoes
4 sweater   T-shirt   coat

5 ★★☆ **Write answers to the questions so they are true for you.**

1 What color is your favorite shirt?
_____

2 What clothes do you love wearing on the weekend?
_____

3 What clothes do you never buy?
_____

4 Of all the people you know, who wears really nice clothes? What do they wear?
_____

Pronunciation

Intonation: listing items

Go to page 120. 🔊

READING

1 REMEMBER AND CHECK **Answer the questions. Then look at the Tweets on page 75 of the Student's Book and check your answers.**

0 (9:44) What are Alex and his mom doing? *They are shopping.*

1 What is he listening to? _____

2 (9:47) A woman is sitting on a chair. What instrument is she playing?

_____

3 (9:48) Is the woman alone? _____

4 (9:49) Do the people in the supermarket like the music? _____

5 (9:53) What are people using to record the concert? _____

6 (9:53) How many girls are dancing? _____

7 (9:55) Who is leaving the supermarket? _____

2 **Read this dialogue from a TV show. How many places does Stella visit in the studios?** _____

STELLA	Hi, everyone. Welcome to today's show. I'm at Stardust Movie Studios. They're making a movie here, and Paolo Mongini, the star of the movie, is showing me around. Thanks a lot, Paolo.
PAOLO	No problem! I like showing people the place. So, first we're going to the studio where we make the movies.
STELLA	There are a lot of people here. What are they all doing?
PAOLO	Well, we aren't shooting this afternoon. They're getting ready for tomorrow. We're shooting in an office, so they're cleaning and tidying the desks, and putting out chairs. Those people are checking the lights.
STELLA	Where next?
PAOLO	OK. This is the room for the clothes. We call it "wardrobe."
STELLA	Wow! Look at all the beautiful dresses and pants and hats and everything. It's very neat.
PAOLO	Yes, each piece of clothing has the actor's name on it. Now, we can't go in this next room, but we can look through the window. You can see young actors.
STELLA	Yes, they're all sitting at desks, like in a classroom. Are they learning their words for tomorrow?
PAOLO	No, it really is a classroom. They're studying math and science.
STELLA	Why?
PAOLO	Well, these kids are still in school. So they shoot in the mornings and have their classes in the afternoons. It's very important.
STELLA	Oh, right. Where next?
PAOLO	The restaurant. I want a cup of coffee. And then we can see some more.
STELLA	Great!

3 **Read the dialogue again and mark the sentences T (true) or F (false). Correct the false statements.**

0 Stella and Paolo both work in TV. [F] *Paolo works in movies.*

1 Paolo likes showing people round the studios. [ ] _____

2 Paolo shows Stella the studio first. [ ] _____

3 There are actors shooting in the studio. [ ] _____

4 The costumes have the movie's name on them. [ ] _____

5 The young actors in the classroom are studying for the movie shoot tomorrow. [ ] _____

6 The young actors have classes every afternoon. [ ] _____

7 Stella and Paolo are going to the restaurant for lunch. [ ] _____

DEVELOPING WRITING

Describing a scene

1 Read Nicole's diary entry. Who calls the writer?

Sunday
May
30

My Sunday afternoon

It's Sunday afternoon. The sun is shining. I'm sitting in the park. I love sitting here. It's quiet and I like watching other people.

There are some children here. They're laughing and playing games. There are four people together near the big tree. They're sitting on the grass. They're having a picnic. They're having fun.

Me? I'm relaxing. It's Sunday! I have my phone with me, and my headphones. I'm listening to music – my favorite music. In my head, I'm singing the song. I'm having a good time here.

Uh-oh! Now my phone's ringing. It's my friend Steve. What does he want?

2 Match the parts of the phrases. Then read the diary entry again and check.

0	watching	*b*
1	playing	
2	having	
3	listening	
4	singing	

a   a song
b   other people
c   games
d   to music
e   fun

3 Imagine it is Sunday afternoon. Use the ideas below and make notes.

1   Choose a place:
  ● the mall
  ● the beach
  ● your house
  ● another place

2   What are you doing? What is happening near you? Who can you see and what are they doing? Use the verbs in the list to help you.

buy | have | listen | play | read | sit | watch

_____
_____
_____
_____
_____
_____
_____
_____

3   Something happens – it changes things. What happens?

_____
_____
_____
_____
_____
_____
_____
_____

4 Use your notes to complete the text about your Sunday afternoon.

It's Sunday afternoon. I'm _____ .
_____ are
_____
_____
_____ .
I'm _____
_____
_____ .
Uh-oh! Now _____
_____
_____ .

LISTENING

1 🔊33 **Listen to a boy calling home from his vacation and answer the questions.**

1 Where is he? _____

2 Where is he going after the call?

_____

2 🔊33 **Listen again and complete the sentences with one word.**

0 The boy's name is _____Rick_____ .

1 It's seven o'clock in the _____ .

2 The boys playing soccer are wearing _____ and _____ .

3 Two _____ are _____ bikes.

4 He thinks the men are going to _____ .

5 The women are _____ dresses and _____ .

6 The children in the _____ are _____ .

7 The boy is _____ to the _____ now.

DIALOGUE

1 🔊34 **Listen to Philip interviewing Julia for a school project. How many questions does he ask?**

2 🔊34 **Listen again and complete the dialogue.**

PHILIP   Hi, Julia! Can I ask you some questions?

JULIA   Yeah, sure. What about?

PHILIP   What do you like doing in the evenings?

JULIA   You mean, after school? Well, I like 0 _____watching TV_____ and I love 1 _____ .

PHILIP   And how about on the weekends?

JULIA   On Saturdays, I help Mom in the kitchen. I like 2 _____ , but I hate 3 _____ the dishes. And on Sundays, I like 4 _____ my friends at the mall and 5 _____ to the movies.

PHILIP   Thanks, Julia. Now I can finish my school project.

3 Now Philip is interviewing his grandfather. Put Grandpa's answers in the correct order.

PHILIP   Grandpa, can I ask you some questions, please?

GRANDPA   Yes, of course. What do you want to know?

PHILIP   Well, what do you like doing in the evenings?

GRANDPA   0   magazines / I / my / reading / love

     I love reading my magazines.

PHILIP   And what about the weekends?

GRANDPA   1   On / I / at / the club / my / Saturdays / like / friends / meeting

     _____

     2   I / On / visit / usually / Sundays / you

     _____

     3   family / seeing / I / your / love

     _____

     4   I / don't / your music / listening / to / like / But / always

     _____

PHILIP   Thanks a lot, Grandpa.

4 Imagine that Philip is interviewing you. Complete the answers to his questions so they are true for you.

PHILIP   What do you like doing in the evenings?

YOU   I like _____ and I love _____ .

PHILIP   How about weekends?

YOU   On Saturday I like _____ and on Sunday I like _____ .

PHILIP   What do you hate doing?

YOU   I hate _____ .

PHILIP   And what are you doing now?

YOU   I'm _____ .

▮▮▮ TRAIN TO THiNK ▮▮▮

Memorizing

1 🔊33   a   Read the questions 1–5.
     b   Cover the questions and listen to Rick.
     c   Answer the questions.
     d   Listen to Rick again and check what you remembered.

1 There are _____ girls playing beach volleyball.

2 There are _____ boys playing soccer.

3 The men on bikes are wearing _____ and _____ .

4 There are _____ children in the ocean.

5 There are _____ boys surfing.

EXAM SKILLS: Reading

Answering multiple-choice questions

1 Read Monica's email to her friend Jodie and answer the questions.

1 Where is Monica? _____

2 What does she want to see there? _____

Hi, Jodie,

How are you? I'm on vacation – well, you know that, right? – and I'm having a great time here in Granada. We're staying in a nice hotel near the city center. It's small, but it's very comfortable, and it isn't expensive. We like it. The people who work here speak good English. That's great because my family doesn't speak Spanish! Well, I know a few words now – *gracias* and *por favor*, that kind of thing! I can say *tengo hambre*, too. (That means "I'm hungry," and you know me, I'm always hungry!)

Granada is a cool place. The famous Alhambra palace is here. It's very beautiful. And it's a great place for Flamenco, too. I love Flamenco dancing and I want to see some. Oh, wait – my mom says that Dad is on his tablet, and he's getting tickets for a Flamenco show tonight here in the city! Great!

Hope you're well. Please write soon, OK?

Adios

Monica

---

2 Read the email again. Choose the correct answers (A, B, or C).

0 Monica's family is staying in a _____ hotel.

  A big   **(B)** comfortable   C expensive

1 The people at the hotel _____ English.

  A like   B don't understand   C understand

2 Monica knows _____ words in Spanish.

  A a few   B a lot of   C no

3 In Granada there is a famous _____ .

  A palace   B dance clubs   C cool place

4 Monica's _____ has a tablet.

  A father   B mother   C Flamenco

5 Monica's father _____ tickets for a Flamenco show.

  A isn't getting   B is buying   C is selling

Reading tip

When the questions about a text are multiple-choice, you have to choose the one correct answer from three or four options.

- Look for items that are grammatically wrong. For example, in the following question, A is wrong because we can't use "a" before a vowel, and C is wrong because we can't use "some" before a singular noun:
- He's eating _____ apple.

  A a   **B** an   **C** some

- Look for words that have similar meanings. For example, in Question 5 of Exercise 2, "buying" and "getting" have the same meaning.
- You have to check all three or four options before you decide which the correct one is.

CONSOLIDATION

LISTENING

1 🔊 35 **Listen to Daniela and (circle) the correct answers (A, B, or C).**

1 Daniela's birthday is …
   A October 20.
   B October 21.
   C October 1.

2 Daniela's camera is a gift from …
   A her grandparents.
   B her brother.
   C her mother and father.

3 Daniela's favorite season is …
   A winter.
   B fall.
   C summer.

2 🔊 35 **Listen again and complete the words.**

1 Daniela is f_____ .
2 She thinks Teaneck isn't e_____ .
3 Daniela is taking d_____ classes.
4 Daniela has special s_____ for dancing.
5 Daniela's friends like s_____ .
6 Daniela likes w_____ on cold days.

GRAMMAR

3 (Circle) **the correct options.**

SILVIA   Hi, Alex. What ¹*are / is* you doing?

ALEX   Oh hi, Silvia. ²*I wait / I'm waiting* for my bus. And you?

SILVIA   I'm doing some shopping. I'm not ³*buying / buy* much – just some food. Hey, you have headphones. Cool!

ALEX   Oh, yeah. ⁴*I'm listening / I listen* to some music. I mean, waiting for the bus is boring! I ⁵*can't / don't can* wait without music!

SILVIA   What ⁶*do you listen / are you listening* to right now?

ALEX   It's some piano music. I really like ⁷*listen / listening* to piano music.

SILVIA   ⁸*Can you / Do you can* play the piano, Alex?

ALEX   No, I ⁹*can't / can*. But I always ¹⁰*listen / am listening* to it!

4 ★★☆ **Fred is showing Lily a video on his phone. Put the words in order to make sentences.**

0 is / Alice / sister / This / my
  This is my sister Alicia.

1 driving / She / her car / is
  _____

2 is / a senior center / She / going to
  _____

3 is / at the retirement home / She / giving / a concert
  _____

4 She's / some / the guitar / of her friends / playing / with
  _____

5 a chair / is / on / Alicia / sitting
  _____

6 next to / is / her / My brother Pedro / standing
  _____

7 Beatles / singing / songs / They're / old
  _____

8 are / The / with / them / seniors / singing
  _____

VOCABULARY

5 **Put the words in the list into three categories. Give each category a title. Then write one more word in each category.**

August | dress | February | golf | gymnastics | jeans
sweater | June | May | surfing | tennis | sneakers

1 *months*	2	3

6 **Complete the sentences with the words in the list. There are two extra words.**

cheer | dance | dancing | second | summer
talk | two | watching

1 My birthday is the _____ of September.
2 I have a problem with my leg, so I can't _____ tonight.
3 I _____ to my friends on the phone every day.
4 I like listening to music, but I don't like _____ to it.
5 We always _____ when our team wins a game.
6 It's great here in the _____ when the weather is hot.

DIALOGUE

7 Put the dialogues in order.

Dialogue 1

	TANYA	No, I don't like watching TV. It's all sport and stuff.
	TANYA	No, it's seven o'clock. The stores close at seven thirty.
1	TANYA	I'm really bored.
	CARLOS	Me, too. Why don't we go downtown? We can go shopping.
	CARLOS	That's right. OK, let's watch TV then.

Dialogue 2

	STEVE	OK, it's no big deal. We can stay here in the house. I have a good book to read.
	STEVE	Hey, how about going for a walk?
	STEVE	Yes, I'm sure I can find one for you.
	DORA	Good idea. I like reading. Do you have a book for me, too?
	DORA	No, thanks! It's cold outside. And I don't like walking very much.

READING

8 Read the phone dialogue. Then complete the sentences with the correct information.

RON	Hey, Mara. What are you doing?
MARA	I'm talking to you on the phone, ha, ha!
RON	Yes, very funny. But seriously – what are you doing?
MARA	Nothing really. I'm just sitting in my room. Why?
RON	How about coming to the park? That's where I am now!
MARA	The park? Why? What's happening in the park?
RON	There's a race today. It's a ten-kilometer run. My parents are running in it.
MARA	Are they crazy? It's winter! It's cold and it's raining.
RON	It isn't raining very much. And I'm wearing a warm coat. So I'm OK.
MARA	Well, no thanks. I like being warm, not cold.
RON	OK, it's no big deal. Oh, I can see Pablo Diaz. He's running in the race, too.
MARA	Really? Pablo from our school?
RON	Yes, him. And he's first – he's winning!
MARA	OK, I'm putting my coat on and I'm leaving the house now.
RON	Really?
MARA	Yes – Pablo Diaz is there, so I want to be there, too!
RON	Oh, OK. See you soon then!

1 Mara is in _____ .

2 Ron is in _____ .

3 There's a _____ -kilometer race today.

4 Ron's _____ and _____ are running in the race.

5 Ron _____ cold because he's _____ a warm coat.

6 Mara doesn't like _____ .

7 Pablo Diaz is a boy from their _____ .

8 Pablo is _____ the race.

9 Mara is _____ the house because she wants to _____ .

WRITING

9 Write a short dialogue between two friends. Use these ideas to help you.

- one friend is bored
- the other friend suggests something to do
- the first friend doesn't like the idea very much
- the second friend suggests another thing to do (go for a walk, go to the movies, play video games, etc.)

9 | WOULD YOU LIKE DESSERT?

GRAMMAR

must / must not `SB page 86`

1 ★☆☆ **Complete the sentences with *must* or *must not*.**

My soccer coach has very strict rules for our team:

0   You ___must not___ drink too much soda.

1   You _____ eat more salad.

2   You _____ eat chocolate or candy before meals.

3   You _____ go to bed late.

4   You _____ come to practice every day after school.

5   You _____ drink lots of water.

2 ★★☆ **Circle the correct options.**

0   A   Do you want to come to my house after school?

   B   I can't. I have a piano lesson tomorrow, so I **must** / *must not* practice tonight.

1   A   Do we have soccer practice today?

   B   Oh, that's right, we do! We *must / must not* remember to bring the right soccer shoes, too. The coach gets really angry when we forget them.

2   A   What a cute dog! Can we take it home?

   B   OK, but it *must / must not* stay outside all the time. You know that dogs make your sister sneeze.

3   A   I'm not ready yet, Dad.

   B   Hurry up! You *must / must not* be there when the bus comes. The driver doesn't wait.

4   A   I want to cook dinner tonight, Mom.

   B   OK, but you *must / must not* wash your hands well before you touch any food.

3 ★★★ **Complete the school rules with *must* (✓) or *must not* (✗) and a verb from the list.**

~~arrive~~ | be | bring | buy | drink | eat | finish
forget | give | sit | talk | wash | write

School Rules

0   Students (✓) ___must arrive___ at school by 8:15 on regular school days.

1   Students (✗) _____ late for class. They (✓) _____ in their seats before the bell rings.

2   Students (✓) _____ their homework before class starts.

3   Teachers (✗) _____ students time for homework in class. Homework is for home!

4   Everyone (✓) _____ their hands before lunch.

5   Students (✗) _____ or _____ in classrooms. Keep all food in the lunchroom.

6   Students (✓) _____ their lunch from home or _____ a boxed lunch. You (✗) _____ to bring $3 for a boxed lunch. No money, no food!

7   Students (✗) _____ on any walls.

4 ★★★ **Write five things you *must* or *must not* do this year.**

0   *I must learn some new English words.*

1   _____

2   _____

3   _____

4   _____

5   _____

can (asking for permission) `SB page 87`

5 ★★☆ **Put the words in order to make questions.**

0   we / Can / the soccer game / Saturday / on / go / to
   Can we go to the soccer game on Saturday ?

1   have / I / Can / an egg / breakfast / for
   _____ ?

2   we / Can / invite / Tom / to / my birthday party
   _____ ?

3   go / we / Can / the movies / to / school / after
   _____ ?

4   call / I / Can / my mom
   _____ ?

6 ★★☆ Match the children's questions with Dad's answers. Draw lines.

0 Can I take your laptop to school with me?

1 Can we go swimming on Saturday?

2 Can I go to Karen's after school tonight?

3 Can Mike and I go climbing this weekend?

a No, we can't. The pool is closed this weekend.

b Yes, of course you can. But don't come home late.

c Well, OK. But be careful.

d No, you can't. I need it for work.

I'd like … / Would you like …? SB page 89

7 ★☆☆ Write sentences using would/I'd like.

0 I / vegetable soup
I'd like vegetable soup.

1 my mom / steak and fries
_____

2 what / you / for dessert / ?
_____

3 Dad / ice cream for dessert / ?
_____

8 ★★☆ Put the dialogue in order.

☐ WAITER (five minutes later) Are you ready to order?

☐ WAITER Four soups, OK. And what would you like for the main course?

☐ WAITER And finally, any drinks?

☐ WAITER OK, so would you like an appetizer?

1 WAITER Good evening. Would you like a table for four?

☐ CUSTOMER Yes, please.

☐ CUSTOMER Yes, we are.

☐ CUSTOMER Just water for everyone.

☐ CUSTOMER We'd like one chicken salad, one steak and fries, one pizza, and one burger with fries and salad, please.

☐ CUSTOMER Yes, please. We'd like two tomato soups and two vegetable soups.

Pronunciation

Intonation: giving two choices
Go to page 121.

9 ★★★ Look at the menu on page 88 of the Student's Book and complete the dialogue so it is true for you.

WAITER Are you ready to order?
YOU Yes, I am.
WAITER Would you like an appetizer?
YOU Yes, please. _____
WAITER And what would you like for the main course?
YOU _____
WAITER And would you like a dessert?
YOU Yes, please. _____
WAITER Any drinks?
YOU Yes, _____

GET IT RIGHT!

like and would like

We use *like* to say that something is nice.
✓ *I like ice cream. It's yummy!*

We use *would like* to ask for something we want or to ask somebody what they want.
✓ *I would like some ice cream, please.*
✗ ~~I like~~ *some ice cream, please.*
✓ *Would you like some ice cream?*
✗ ~~You like~~ *some ice cream?*

Circle the correct options.

0 I *like* / *would like* to come to your house tomorrow.
1 I *like* / *would like* a dog for my birthday.
2 I *like* / *would like* this house and I'm happy living here.
3 I *like* / *would like* to wear a warmer coat today. It's cold.
4 I *like* / *would like* to go shopping on Monday. Can I go?
5 I'm thirsty. I *like* / *would like* a drink of water.
6 When I have time, I *like* / *would like* reading.

VOCABULARY

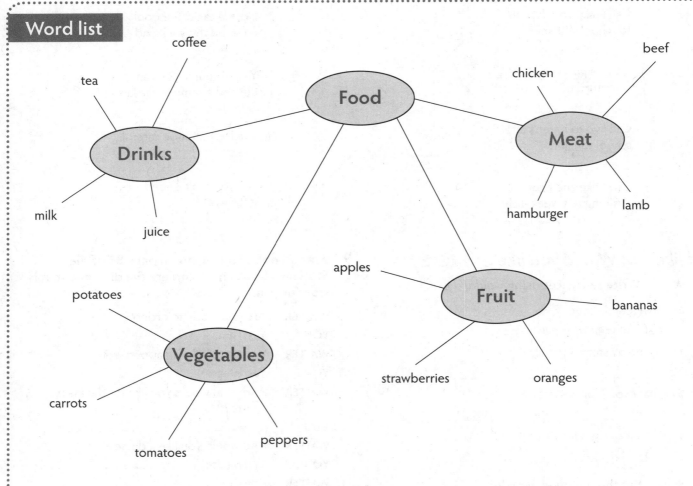

coffee

tea

Food

chicken

beef

Drinks

Meat

milk

juice

hamburger

lamb

potatoes

apples

Fruit

bananas

Vegetables

carrots

strawberries

oranges

tomatoes

peppers

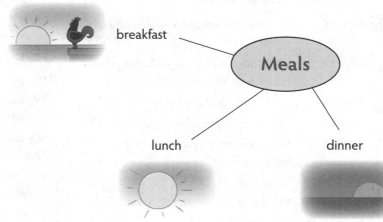

breakfast

Meals

lunch

dinner

Key words in context

a little	There is only **a little** cheese in the fridge.
appetizer	Would you like an **appetizer**?
be careful	**Be careful.** Don't spill the coffee.
borrow	Can I **borrow** your laptop? Mine is broken.
butter	I like **butter** and jam on my toast.
cereal	I usually have **cereal** with milk for breakfast.
dessert	I'd like chocolate ice cream for **dessert**.
honey	I often have bread and **honey** for breakfast.
menu	Great. There's pizza on the **menu** today.
order	Are you ready to **order**?

Food and drink `SB page 86`

1 ★☆☆ **Look at the pictures and complete the puzzle. What's the mystery sentence?**

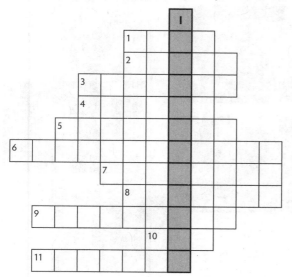

The mystery sentence is:

_____

2 ★★☆ **Unscramble the words and complete the sentences.**

0 We're having _____*beef*_____ with potatoes and vegetables for lunch today. (e b e f)

1 My mom doesn't like _____ . (g e s s a u s a)

2 I often drink _____ with my breakfast. (l i m k)

3 I sometimes have an _____ after dinner. (p l p a e)

4 I'd like _____ and ice cream for dessert. (s t a r w b i r r e e s)

5 I like most vegetables, but I don't like _____ . (a c o r r t s)

Meals `SB page 89`

3 ★☆☆ **Find and (circle) nine breakfast items in the word snake.**

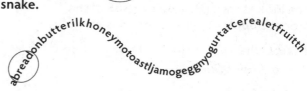

abreadonbutterilkhoneymotoastljamogeggnyogurtatcerealetfruitth

4 ★★☆ **Put the words in order to make sentences.**

0 you / do / usually / eat / for / breakfast, / What / Mara / ?
What do you usually eat for breakfast, Mara?

1 always / I / eat / an / egg / breakfast / for
_____

2 usually / I / eat / toast
_____

3 you / lunch / usually / have / for / What / do / ?
_____

4 often / I / have / salad / a
_____

5 sometimes / have / I / steak / fries / vegetables / and / with
_____

6 do / you / What / usually / drink / meals, / with / your / Mara / ?
_____

7 drink / I / usually / or water / juice
_____

8 never / I / drink / coffee
_____

5 ★★☆ **Check (✓) the things Mara has for breakfast and lunch in Exercise 4.**

☐ fruit   ☐ toast   ☐ an egg
☐ water   ☐ coffee   ☐ pizza
☐ spaghetti   ☐ vegetables   ☐ salad
☐ juice   ☐ yogurt   ☐ cereal
☐ steak   ☐ chicken   ☐ fries

6 ★★★ **Write sentences about Joe and Jamie using the words in parentheses.**

	always	often	sometimes	never
breakfast	eggs	toast	cereal	yogurt
lunch	coffee	a sandwich	pizza	soup
dinner	soup	pasta	fish and chips	salad

0 They _sometimes have cereal for breakfast._ (sometimes)

1 _____ (always)

2 _____ (often)

3 _____ (never)

4 _____ (sometimes)

5 _____ (often)

READING

1 REMEMBER AND CHECK **Answer the questions. Then look at the article on page 85 of the Student's Book and check your answers.**

0 What's the name of the TV show?
Star Junior Chefs

1 How old is Billy?
_____

2 Where is he from?
_____

3 How old must you be to go on the show?
_____

4 What does Billy cook this time?
_____

5 What time does the show end?
_____

2 **Read the brochure for Cooking Camp. What can you learn to make? Check (✓) the correct photos.**

SPRING BREAK COOKING CAMP

April 4—6

Mornings (3 days) 10:00 a.m.–1:00 p.m. (ages 11–14 years) $45 per week

Learn to make CAKES, BREAD, PIZZA, PASTA, HEALTHY SOUPS, & FRUIT SMOOTHIES
Marianne is an excellent cook and she loves good food. She has family in Spain, Turkey, Italy, and Russia. She loves food from all those countries. Come and learn to cook with her.
You must be 11–14 years old.

You must love food.
You must wear a chef's hat.
You must not be late. There's a lot to learn.
And remember! Cooking is fun!

Call 346 555 8165 to reserve a spot.

3 **Read the brochure again. Then correct the sentences.**

0 Cooking Camp is in May.
Cooking Camp is in October.

1 Cooking Camp is for three afternoons.
_____

2 You don't make any drinks.
_____

3 Marianne has family in Brazil.
_____

4 You must be 8–11 years old.
_____

5 You must not wear any special clothes.
_____

6 You must not be on time.
_____

7 Remember that cooking is important.
_____

4 **Complete the questionnaire for Cooking Camp so it is true for you.**

COOKING CAMP QUESTIONNAIRE

1 What's your name? _____

2 How old are you? _____

3 What is your favorite dish? _____

4 Do you help your parents in the kitchen?
_____

5 Can you cook? _____

6 What can you cook? _____
_____

DEVELOPING WRITING

My meal plan

1 Plan three meals for the day. Write your food choices in the columns. Use the words in the list and your own ideas.

bread | burger | cereal | chicken | chocolate
chocolate cake | coffee | cola | eggs | fish
fries | fruit | juice | honey | ice cream
jam | pizza | tea | toast | vegetables
vegetable soup | yogurt

Breakfast	Lunch	Dinner

2 Read about Sam's lunch. Then answer the questions.

I often eat a healthy lunch. I never eat burgers and fries. I always eat salad or vegetables with my meal. For dessert, I usually have fruit. Today it's an apple. But sometimes I eat ice cream. My favorite is strawberry ice cream. I always have a drink with my meal. I usually drink water, but I sometimes have orange juice. I never drink soda.

0 How often does Sam eat burger and fries?
He never eats burgers and fries.

1 What fruit does he have today?

2 What is his favorite ice cream?

3 What does he always have with his meal?

4 What does he usually drink with his meal?

3 Complete the diagram with the words from Exercise 1.

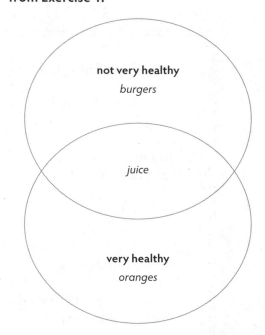

not very healthy
burgers

juice

very healthy
oranges

4 Use your notes in Exercise 3 to complete a healthy meal plan.

Every day, I eat a healthy _____ .
Sometimes I eat _____ and sometimes I eat _____ . I always eat _____ with my meal. I don't like _____ or _____ .
For dessert, I usually have _____ .
But sometimes I eat _____ .
I really like _____ . I usually have a drink with my meal. I usually drink _____ , but I sometimes have _____ . I never drink _____ .

Writing tip

Add more detail to your writing by using adverbs of frequency.
- How often do you eat things?
  You can answer this question with *always*, *usually*, *sometimes*, and *never*.
  I *sometimes* have fish for lunch.
  I *never* drink soda.
  I *usually* have fruit for dessert.
  I *always* have vegetables with my meal.

LISTENING

1 🔊37 Listen and (circle) the correct options to complete the menu.

RIVER PARK CAFÉ

- Menu -

APPETIZERS
¹*Tomato / Carrot* Soup
Vegetable Soup

MAIN COURSE
Steak with ²*fries / vegetables*
Baked potato with ³*chicken / cheese*
⁴*Bean / Chicken* taco
Fish & chips
⁵*Pizza / Pasta* with tomato sauce
Omelette with peppers

DESSERT
⁶*Chocolate / Carrot* cake
⁷*Strawberries / Bananas* & ice cream

DRINKS
⁸*Carrot / Apple* juice
Orange juice
⁹*Soda / Coffee*
Water

2 🔊37 Listen again. Mark the sentences T (true) or F (false).

0 The girl orders chocolate cake for dessert. `F`

1 The boy doesn't like tomatoes. ☐

2 He likes eggs so he orders the omelette. ☐

3 He orders strawberries with ice cream for dessert. ☐

4 She orders coffee to drink. ☐

5 He orders apple juice. ☐

DIALOGUE

1 (Circle) the correct options.

WAITER	Are you ready to ¹*sit down / order*?
CUSTOMER 1	Yes, we are.
WAITER	Would you like ²*an appetizer / a main course*?
CUSTOMER 1	Yes, please. I'd like tomato soup.
CUSTOMER 2	And I'd like vegetable soup.
WAITER	And what would you like for the ³*dessert / main course*?
CUSTOMER 1	I'd like chicken salad, please.
CUSTOMER 2	And I'd like fish and chips, please.
WAITER	And for ⁴*appetizer / dessert*?
CUSTOMER 1	We'd like chocolate cake, please.
WAITER	Any ⁵*drinks / desserts*?
CUSTOMER 1	Yes, please. I'd like apple juice.
CUSTOMER 2	And I'd like water.

PHRASES FOR FLUENCY

SB page 91

1 Complete the dialogues with the phrases in the list.

Of course. | Be careful. | a little | the thing is

Dialogue 1

A Can you take these plates to the table?
B OK.
A _____ Don't drop them.
B I know, Dad.

Dialogue 2

A What's for dinner?
B Pizza.
A Oh, no.
B What's wrong with pizza? I love it.
A Well, _____, I don't like tomatoes.

Dialogue 3

A Is there any chicken in the salad?
B Yes, there is and there's _____ cheese, too.

Dialogue 4

A Would you like butter on your potato?
B _____ A potato must have butter.

Sum it up

1   Unscramble the letters to find the food.

What's on Paul's pizza?

0	s e e c h e	*cheese*
1	r e p s p e p	_____
2	k i c e n c h	_____
3	o e s t o m t a	_____

What would Sally like for dinner?

4	k e a s t	_____
5	t o p o e s t a	_____
6	d a s a l	_____

What's in David's dessert?

7	c o c h l a t e o	_____
8	c i e r e c a m	_____
9	r a w s t e r r i e b s	_____
10	n a b a n a	_____

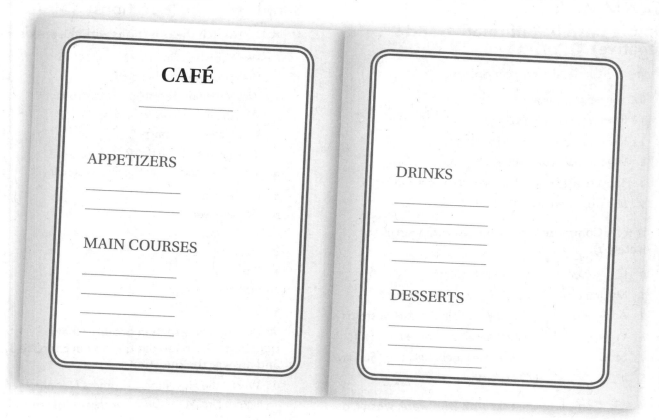

CAFÉ

APPETIZERS

MAIN COURSES

DRINKS

DESSERTS

2   Write a menu. Use food and drink words from the unit.

- Think of a name for your café.
- Create a milkshake or a smoothie.
- Make a special pizza for your café.
- Create meals with the food words.
- Create one unusual meal.

For example: *Strawberry and Orange Salad* or *Carrot and Orange Soup*

3   Imagine you have a customer at your café. Complete the dialogue.

WAITER   Hello and welcome to _____ Café.

CUSTOMER 1   Hello. We'd like a table for two.

WAITER   OK. Follow me, please.

(5 minutes later)

WAITER   Are you ready to order now?

CUSTOMER 1   Yes, we are.

WAITER   Would you like an appetizer?

CUSTOMER 1   Yes, please. I _____ and my friend _____ .

WAITER   And what _____ for the main course?

CUSTOMER 1   _____ , please.

CUSTOMER 2   And _____ .

WAITER   And for dessert?

CUSTOMER 1   _____ , please.

CUSTOMER 2   And _____ .

WAITER   Any drinks?

CUSTOMER 1   Yes, please. _____ for me, and for my friend _____ .

10 | HIGH FLIERS

GRAMMAR

Simple past: *be* (affirmative and negative) `SB page 94`

1 ★☆☆ (Circle) the correct options.

0 You *was* / (*were*) late.

1 It *wasn't* / *weren't* his dog.

2 I *was* / *were* at home yesterday.

3 We *was* / *were* at a baseball game.

4 They *wasn't* / *weren't* at the movies last night.

5 She *was* / *were* my best friend.

2 ★★☆ Complete the sentences with *was(n't)* or *were(n't)*.

0 I _____*was*_____ (✓) born in Houston.

1 My grandma _____ (✗) an astronaut.

2 Andy and Jay _____ (✓) in the park yesterday.

3 We _____ (✗) at my aunt's house last night.

4 Leon _____ (✗) at the baseball game on Sunday.

5 It _____ (✓) my birthday yesterday.

3 ★★★ Complete the text with *was, were, wasn't,* or *weren't*.

The Montgolfier brothers
⁰_____*were*_____ the inventors
of the hot-air balloon. They
¹_____ (✓) French. Their
names ²_____ (✓) Joseph-
Michel and Jacques-Étienne.
Joseph-Michel ³_____
(✓) born in 1740, and Jacques-
Étienne ⁴_____ (✓) born
in 1745. There ⁵_____ (✓) sixteen children in
the family. Their father ⁶_____ (✗) an inventor.
He ⁷_____ (✓) a paper manufacturer.

The first balloon flight ⁸_____ (✓) in June 1783.
There ⁹_____ (✗) any passengers. There
¹⁰_____ (✓) no one on the balloon. The second
flight ¹¹_____ (✓) in Paris in September 1783.
This time, there ¹²_____ (✓) three passengers,
but the passengers ¹³_____ (✗) people. They
¹⁴_____ (✓) a chicken, a duck, and a sheep.

Simple past: *be* (questions) `SB page 95`

4 ★☆☆ Match the questions with the answers.

0 Were you born in Texas? `e`

1 Was your grandfather a chef?

2 Was Valentina Tereshkova an astronaut?

3 Was the noise from your class?

4 Was I late to the party?

5 Were you and I on time?

6 Were Sam and Joe at the mall yesterday?

a No, he wasn't.

b Yes, you were!

c Yes, it was.

d No, we weren't.

e Yes, I was.

f No, they weren't.

g Yes, she was.

5 ★★☆ Put the words in order to make questions. Then look at the text in Exercise 3 and answer the questions.

0 Were / the / inventors / brothers / Montgolfier
   Were the Montgolfier brothers inventors?
   Yes, they were.

1 they / Spanish / Were

   _____

   _____

2 Was / Joseph-Michel / in 1740 / born

   _____

   _____

3 Was / inventor / an / their / father

   _____

   _____

4 the / Was / in / flight / first / June 1795

   _____

   _____

5 flight / second / Prague / in / Was / the

   _____

   _____

6 Were / there / passengers / any

   _____

   _____

Simple past: regular verbs `SB page 97`

6 ★☆☆ **Complete the table with the simple past form of the verbs in the list.**

believe | carry | cry | finish | help
like | live | study | ~~work~~

+ -ed	+ -d	+ -ied
worked		

7 ★★☆ **Put the words in order to make sentences. Put the verbs in the simple past.**

0   uncle / My / study / college / in / medicine
    My uncle studied medicine in college.

1   finish / studies / his / He / 2010 / in
    _____

2   at / hospital / a / He / work / Atlanta / in
    _____

3   in / He / Tampa / three / years / for / live
    _____

4   like / He / the U.S. / very / much
    _____

5   move / He / Rio de Janeiro / to / 2014 / in
    _____

8 ★★☆ **Complete the sentences with the simple past form of the verbs in parentheses.**

> **Name:** Weather Girl
> **Profession:** Superhero TV Presenter
> **Powers:** She can change the weather.

Weather Girl 0 _____*lived*_____ (live) in Toronto. She 1_____ (study) geography in college. She 3_____ (work) for TV Canada. One night, she 3_____ (walk) home in the rain. Suddenly, a car 4_____ (crash) into a wall. Weather Girl 5_____ (call) for an ambulance. They 6_____ (wait) for the ambulance in the rain. It was wet and cold. "Please stop the rain," she 7_____ (cry). Suddenly, the clouds 8_____ (move) away, and there was no more rain. That night, Weather Girl 9_____ (discover) her super powers.

Pronunciation

Simple past: regular verbs

Go to page 121. 🔊

9 ★★☆ **Complete the text with the simple past form of the verbs in parentheses.**

Florence Nightingale

Florence Nightingale 0_____*was*_____ (be) a famous English nurse. She 1_____ (be) born in Florence, Italy, in 1820. Later, her parents 2_____ (move) back to England. As a child, she 3_____ (like) helping others. She 4_____ (care) for sick people and animals. She 5_____ (want) to be a nurse.
In 1851, she 6_____ (work) as a nurse in Germany. In 1853, there 7_____ (be) a war. It 8_____ (be) called the Crimean War. They 9_____ (need) nurses, so Florence 10_____ (travel) with other nurses to help. They 11_____ (care) for the British soldiers there. Life 12_____ (not be) easy. The war 13_____ (end) in 1856. Florence Nightingale 14_____ (return) to England as a hero. She 15_____ (die) in London in 1910.

GET IT RIGHT! 👁

was/wasn't and *were/weren't*

We use *was*, *wasn't*, *were*, and *weren't* to talk about the past. We use *am*, *am not*, *is*, *isn't*, *are*, and *aren't* to talk about now.

✓ Yesterday, **was** my birthday.
✗ Yesterday, ~~is~~ my birthday.

Correct the sentences.

0   Jeff isn't at school yesterday.
    Jeff wasn't at school yesterday.

1   There is a great movie on TV last night.
    _____

2   Hello! I was very happy to see you.
    _____

3   All my friends are there for my birthday last night.
    _____

4   Is Ian with you yesterday evening?
    _____

5   Jemma was worried about her exam today.
    _____

6   They aren't late for school yesterday.
    _____

VOCABULARY

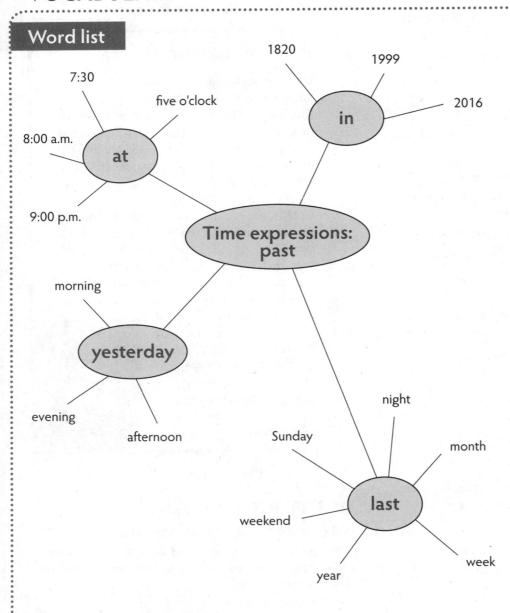

Time expressions: past

at
- 7:30
- five o'clock
- 8:00 a.m.
- 9:00 p.m.

in
- 1820
- 1999
- 2016

yesterday
- morning
- evening
- afternoon

last
- Sunday
- night
- month
- week
- year
- weekend

The weather

It's sunny.

It's hot.

It's snowing.

It's cold.

It's cloudy.

It's raining.

It's windy.

It's warm.

Key words in context

arrive	We **arrived** home at six o'clock.
astronaut	I'd love to be an **astronaut** and fly to the moon.
born	I was **born** in 2002. My birthday is on June 22.
call	My name is Jake, but my mom **calls** me Sonny.
decide	Joe **decided** to go to a different school.
die	Walt Disney **died** in 1966.
flight	We are going to Los Angeles by plane. The **flight** is six hours.
monster	The **monster** in the story has one eye.
space	You need a special plane to travel in **space**.
storm	There was a big **storm** last night.
strange	First it was sunny, then it rained, then it snowed. It was a **strange** day.
work	Annie **worked** in a hospital. She was a doctor.

Time expressions: past `SB page 94`

1 ★☆☆ **Complete the table with the words in the list.**

afternoon | evening | ~~month~~ | morning
night | Saturday | three o'clock | year
6:00 p.m. | 10:30 a.m. | 1999 | 2015

last	in
month	
at	**yesterday**

2 ★☆☆ **Complete the dialogues with *in*, *at*, *yesterday*, and *last*.**

0

A Where were you ____*last*____ night?

B I was at home.

1

A Were you at school _____ afternoon?

B Yes, I was.

2

A Was James at the party _____ Saturday?

B No, he was at home.

3

A Was your dad born _____ 1980?

B No, he wasn't.

4

A Was Tim still at school _____ 5 p.m. this evening?

B Yes, he was.

3 ★★☆ **Where were you? Write sentences with *at*, *last*, and *yesterday* and the time if necessary.**

0 (at) *I was on the bus at eight o'clock.*

1 (at) _____

2 (last) _____

3 (yesterday) _____

The weather `SB page 97`

4 ★★☆ **Complete the crossword.**

ACROSS

4 Today it's _____ , so you don't need sunglasses.

5 It's _____ , so don't forget your umbrella.

7 It's _____ , so it's a great day to fly your kite.

8 It's _____ – there are lots of people on the beach today.

DOWN

1 Today is sunny and _____ . Let's sit outside.

2 Drink a lot of water today – it's very _____ !

3 You can make a snowman today. It's _____ .

4 It's _____ today, so don't forget to wear warm clothes.

5 ★★☆ **Circle the correct options in these dialogues.**

1

A What's the weather like?

B It's [0] *sunny* / *cloudy*. I'm wearing shorts.

A Is it [1] *cold* / *hot*?

B Yes, it is. I'm wearing a T-shirt. What's the weather like there?

A It's very [2] *cloudy* / *windy* here. Listen. Can you hear it?

B Yes, I can.

2

A What's the weather like?

B It's [3] *raining* / *cloudy*. I can't go running outside today.

A Is it [4] *cold* / *hot*?

B Yes, it is. I'm wearing a sweater and a coat. What's the weather like there?

A It's [5] *snowing* / *windy* here. We can't go to school today because we can't get out of the house.

B Really?

6 ★★★ **Write a sentence about the weather today.**

_____

READING

1 **REMEMBER AND CHECK** **Answer the questions. Then look at the article on page 93 of the Student's Book and check your answers.**

    0   Where was Valentina Tereshkova born?   *She was born in Russia.*

    1   What was her mother's job?   _____

    2   What was Valentina's job?   _____

    3   What was her hobby?   _____

    4   When was her first flight in space?   _____

    5   How many days was she in space?   _____

    6   What was her face on?   _____

    7   When did she carry the Olympic flag?   _____

2 **Read the article about the superhero *Weather Girl*. Find and write the words.**

    1   a season: _____

    2   three weather words: _____ _____ _____

Weather Girl

Her real name is Milly Moon but people call her Weather Girl. They call her that because she can control the weather. (**A**) She can control the clouds and the wind. When Weather Girl uses her powers, she saves people's lives. She's a superhero.

Milly Moon was born on December 31, 1995. It was winter, and it was a cold and windy day. That night, there was a big snow storm. Mr. and Mrs. Moon walked home with their new baby girl. (**B**) But baby Milly wasn't cold. She was warm. Her parents were surprised. "She's a very special baby," they decided. And they were right.

Milly Moon lived with her parents and her sister in a small town in Canada. When she was 16, she used her special powers for the first time. One day, there was a lot of snow. It was her sister Jojo's birthday. Jojo was very sad. She wanted a party, but there was too much snow. Milly Moon looked out of the window at the snow. She closed her eyes and counted to ten. Then she opened them. (**C**) "Look Jojo! You can have your party now." Jojo was happy again.

Milly was always interested in the weather. She studied geography in college. (**D**) She studied the weather day and night. One night, there was a lot of rain, so much that it filled people's houses. (**E**) Now, Milly often uses her special powers and she helps a lot of people.

3 **Read the article again. Match the sentences with the correct places (A–E).**

    0   Suddenly, there wasn't any snow.   `C`

    1   Then she worked at a local TV station as a weather girl.   ☐

    2   She can make rain or snow.   ☐

    3   They were very cold, and they nearly died.   ☐

    4   Weather Girl stopped the rain and saved four people's lives.   ☐

DEVELOPING WRITING

A short biography

1   Use the information in the list to complete the factfile.

actor | American | ~~Christopher Reeve~~
four Superman movies | New York City
September 25, 1952 | the superhero, Superman
52 | 1978 | 1987 | 2004

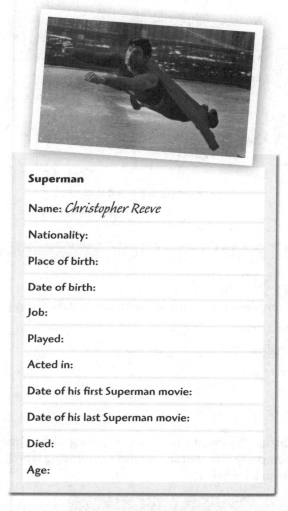

Superman

Name: *Christopher Reeve*

Nationality:

Place of birth:

Date of birth:

Job:

Played:

Acted in:

Date of his first Superman movie:

Date of his last Superman movie:

Died:

Age:

2   Look at Exercise 1 and complete the short biography.

Christopher Reeve was an American actor. He was born in [1]_____ on [2]_____ . He played [3]_____ . He acted in [4]_____ . His first Superman movie was in [5]_____ and his last movie was in [6]_____ . He died in [7]_____ . He was [8]_____ years old.

3   Look at the notes about Spider-Man and Tobey Maguire. Then use the notes to write a short biography of him.

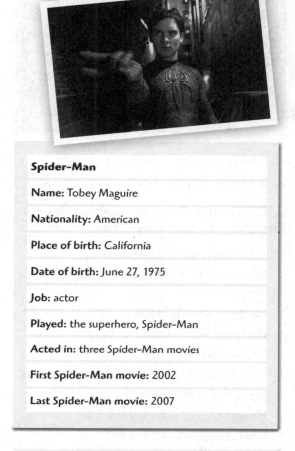

Spider–Man

Name: Tobey Maguire

Nationality: American

Place of birth: California

Date of birth: June 27, 1975

Job: actor

Played: the superhero, Spider–Man

Acted in: three Spider–Man movies

First Spider–Man movie: 2002

Last Spider–Man movie: 2007

LISTENING

1 Look at the photo and guess the answers to the questions.

1 Who is the man in the photo? _____

2 What did he write about? _____

2 🔊40 Listen to Tom talking about his hero. Circle the the correct options.

0 Tom's hero was a (writer) / artist.

1 His most famous book was *Huckleberry Finn* / *The Jungle Book*.

2 His parents were *English* / *Indian*.

3 His father was *a doctor* / *an artist*.

4 Rudyard Kipling *loved* / *hated* India.

5 He was *happy* / *unhappy* with the Holloways.

6 He *loved* / *hated* books.

7 He was *happy* / *unhappy* at school.

8 After school he lived in *Italy* / *India*.

9 He worked for a *newspaper* / *university*.

3 🔊40 Listen again and complete the text with the correct words.

Rudyard Kipling's parents were English. They ⁰ __*moved*__ to India. His father was an artist, and he worked at a School of Art in Mumbai. Kipling loved India. He loved the ¹_____ and the culture. However, he didn't have a happy childhood. His parents wanted him to go to ²_____ in England. When he was six years old, he lived with a ³_____ , the Holloways in a small ⁴_____ in England. Mrs. Holloway was very bad to him. He ⁵_____ life there, and he was very unhappy. Luckily, he ⁶_____ books. He loved books. They ⁷_____ him from his unhappy life.

DIALOGUE

1 Complete the dialogue with the simple past of the verbs in parentheses. Then put the dialogue in order.

1	BEN	⁰ __*Were*__ (be) you at home yesterday?
☐	BEN	¹_____ it a good party?
☐	BEN	Did they? ²_____ (be) they good?
☐	BEN	Oh, I remember. It ³_____ (be) your cousin's birthday yesterday, right?
☐	SAM	Yes, it ⁴_____ (be). I loved it.
☐	SAM	No, I ⁵_____ (not be). I ⁶_____ (be) at my cousin's house.
☐	SAM	Yes, they ⁷_____ (be) very good.
☐	SAM	Yes, it ⁸_____ (be). Her brothers are in a band. They ⁹_____ (play) at her party.

▰ TRAIN TO THiNK ▰

Sequencing

1 Complete the sequence with the words in the list.

And then

Finally

First

_____ > Then > _____ > After that > _____

2 Order the events in Rudyard Kipling's life. Then complete the sentences with sequencing words from Exercise 1.

Rudyard Kipling (1865–1936)

☐	_____ he died in London in 1936.
☐	_____ he lived in a small town in England with the Holloway family.
1	__*First*__ Rudyard Kipling lived in India.
☐	_____ he moved to a school in Devon.
☐	_____ he moved back to India and he worked for a newspaper.

Listening for key words

1 🔊41 **Listen and check (✓) the months you hear.**

January ☐ | February ☐ | March ☐ | April ☐ | May ☐ | June ☐ | July ☐
August ☐ | September ☐ | October ☐ | November ☐ | December ☐

Listening tip

- First, learn to listen for key words, for example, the months of the year.
- Next, you need to complete the profile. Listen carefully for the dates, the jobs, and the places.

Remember! You don't need to understand everything.

---

2 🔊42 **Listen and circle the correct options to complete Norman Rockwell's profile.**

Norman Rockwell

0 Job
writer / (*painter*)

1 Nationality
American / British

2 Born
February 3 / January 3 in 1894

3 Father's job
manager / artist

4 Started at Chase Art School
age *13 / 14*

5 Age 21
He moved to *New Rochelle / New York.*

6 1916
He married his *first / second* wife, Irene.

7 Died
December / November 1978

3 🔊43 **Listen and complete Vincent Van Gogh's profile.**

Vincent Van Gogh

0 Job
painter
_____

1 Nationality
_____

2 Born
_____

3 Studied
_____

4 Lived in Paris
_____

5 Lived with
_____

6 Number of paintings sold when alive
_____

7 Age died
_____

8 Date died
_____

9 Famous painting name
_____

CONSOLIDATION

LISTENING

1 🔊44 **Listen to Susie and Jack and (circle) the correct answers (A, B, or C).**

1 For breakfast, Susie doesn't want …
  A orange juice.
  B cereal.
  C eggs.
2 Susie arrived home at …
  A eleven o'clock.
  B twelve o'clock.
  C one o'clock.
3 Susie wants to read her …
  A emails.
  B newspaper.
  C tablet.

2 🔊44 **Listen again. Mark the sentences T (true) or F (false).**

1 Susie wants yogurt for breakfast. ☐
2 She wants milk. ☐
3 Last night, Susie was at a party. ☐
4 Jack worked for five hours last night. ☐
5 Jack says he always works hard. ☐
6 The weather is rainy and cold. ☐
7 Susie wants to borrow Jack's tablet. ☐
8 Susie is going to work. ☐

GRAMMAR

3 **(Circle) the correct options.**

1 Mom, *can / must* I ask you a question?
2 Hurry up! We *must / must not* be late today.
3 Are you hungry? *Would / Do* you like a sandwich?
4 *It / There* wasn't a nice day yesterday. It was cold and rainy.
5 You really *can / must* be careful, John. Don't break it!
6 *Would / Do* you like this music?
7 *It / There* was a good movie on TV last night.
8 Hi. *I like / I'd like* a cup of coffee, please.
9 My friend *wasn't / weren't* at school yesterday.
10 I *study / studied* for the test last night.

4 **Complete the sentences with the correct form of the verbs in the list.**

arrive | be (x2) | like | not be (x2) | rain
show | stay | travel | want | watch

Our vacation last year wasn't very good!
We [1]_____ to the beach in Rhode Island.
We [2]_____ at our hotel very late and the manager
[3]_____ angry with us. Then he [4]_____ us
the rooms. They [5]_____ really small and cold. We
[6]_____ to change the rooms but the manager
said that there [7]_____ any other rooms. We
[8]_____ in the hotel for three days. The weather
[9]_____ good. It [10]_____ almost all the time!
One day we stayed in the room and [11]_____ TV for
five hours. But the food was good. We [12]_____ it a
lot. Next year, we don't want to go to that hotel again.

VOCABULARY

5 **Complete the words.**

1 Do you want black coffee, or coffee with m _ _ k?
2 It's cold and w _ _ _ y today.
3 I don't eat a lot of v _ _ _ _ _ _ _ _ s.
4 My favorite fruits are o _ _ _ _ _ _ s and bananas.
5 I was at the movie theater yesterday e _ _ _ _ _ g.
6 It was his birthday last m _ _ _ h.
7 There's no sun today. It's very c _ _ _ _ _ y.
8 I watched TV yesterday a _ _ _ _ _ _ _ _ n.
9 I'd like orange juice and eggs for b _ _ _ _ _ _ _ t.
10 My favorite meal is a b _ _ _ _ _ with fries.

6 **Complete the dialogue with the words in the list.**

dinner | fruit | meat | night | ~~o'clock~~
potatoes | strawberries | tea

TOM What time do you usually eat in your family?

NICKY Well, we usually have lunch at one [0] _*o'clock*_ .
And then we have [1]_____ at eight in the evening.

TOM And what do you eat in the evening?

NICKY We have [2]_____ – beef or chicken – and some vegetables, for example, carrots or [3]_____ . I usually drink juice, but my parents like hot drinks, so they have [4]_____ .

TOM And then?

NICKY Then we have [5]_____ – usually bananas, but last [6]_____ we had [7]_____ .

DIALOGUE

7 Complete the dialogue with the words in the list. There are two extra words.

bit | can | careful | course | liked | must | thing | wanted | was | wasn't | were | weren't

NINA   So, what was Jason's party like last night?

CHUCK   It was good. We all enjoyed it. There [1]_____ great music and we danced a lot. And all my friends were there.

NINA   Was there any food?

CHUCK   Yes. There [2]_____ sandwiches and cheese, and some great chicken wings, too. The [3]_____ is ...

NINA   Yes?

CHUCK   Well, Jason's mom cooked some chili and it [4]_____ good at all! No one [5]_____ it. She [6]_____ think it's good – she cooked a lot of it! But at the end of the party, it was all still there! I usually love curry, but not that!

NINA   Oh, no. Oh, look. Jason's coming. Be [7]_____! Don't say anything about the chili, OK?

CHUCK   No, sure. Jason! Hi. How are you? Thanks for the party!

JASON   Hi, Chuck. Hi, Nina. No problem. I'm happy that you enjoyed it. But Chuck, [8]_____ I ask you something?

CHUCK   Um, of [9]_____. What?

JASON   My mom's chili. Was it really terrible? No one [10]_____ to eat it!

CHUCK   Go on, Chuck. I think you can tell him!

READING

8 Read Christie's diary entry. Then correct the sentences.

1 Yesterday was Christie's 14th birthday.
   _____

2 The restaurant only serves Italian food.
   _____

3 The restaurant was noisy.
   _____

4 Christie didn't like the tomato soup.
   _____

5 Christie's mother and father don't eat fish.
   _____

6 Christie's family eat in restaurants a lot.
   _____

7 There were words on the candles.
   _____

8 Christie's family is having dinner at a restaurant tonight.
   _____

> March 17th
>
> Yesterday was my birthday, so my family had dinner in a restaurant downtown. It's an Italian restaurant, but they have all kinds of different food there. There weren't a lot of other people in the restaurant, so it was very quiet.
>
> The dinner was really nice. We started with tomato soup – it was delicious! Then I ordered beef with peppers and mushrooms. My parents ordered fish (they don't eat meat) with tomato sauce and rice. And after that, we had ice cream, my favorite. The food was really good – I enjoyed my meal a lot. We don't usually eat in restaurants so it was a special evening.
>
> When we finished dinner, a waiter came over with a birthday cake! It had 13 candles on it (of course!) and "Happy Birthday Christie" was in letters on the top of the cake. The waiters and my parents started to sing to me, and the other people in the restaurant joined in, too. At the end of the song, everyone clapped – it was really cool! There was enough cake for us and for the other people in the restaurant, and there's some in the fridge in our kitchen now!
>
> So, dinner tonight at our house is pasta and salad – and birthday cake!

WRITING

9 Write a paragraph about a good or bad meal you remember. Write 35–50 words. Use the questions to help you.

- Where were you?
- What was the meal? (dinner? lunch?)
- Who was there?
- What was the food?
- Why was it a good/bad meal?

11 A WORLD OF ANIMALS

GRAMMAR

Simple past: irregular verbs SB page 104

1 ★☆☆ Complete the table with the simple past or the base form of the verbs.

base form	past
0 run	*ran*
1	came
2	put
3 give	
4 see	
5	knew
6	drank
7 fall	
8 write	
9	took
10 eat	

2 ★★☆ Complete the text with the simple past form of the verbs in parentheses.

The Hill family's vacation

Last year the Hill family from New Jersey decided to go on vacation in Europe. They
⁰ ___*went*___ (go) to the west of England. Mr. Hill ¹_____ (make) a reservation at a hotel in a city called Bath. In Bath they ²_____ (see) old Roman buildings and the city center. Then Patty Hill ³_____ (find) Longleat Safari Park on her computer. She ⁴_____ (tell) her parents about the old house and the park with lions, gorillas, and lots of different animals.
The website ⁵_____ (say) it was the first safari park outside Africa. Everyone ⁶_____ (think) it was a good idea. So they ⁷_____ (get) in the car and ⁸_____ (drive) to Longleat. They ⁹_____ (have) a really good time there!

Simple past (negative) SB page 104

3 ★★★ Write sentences about a birthday party. Use the simple past negative.

0 my grandmother / to the party (come)
  My grandmother didn't come to the party. _____

1 the band / classical music (play)
  _____

2 we / pizza (eat)
  _____

3 Safron / me a dictionary (give)
  _____

4 Mom / my dress (make)
  _____

5 Bobby / the gift from his family (see)
  _____

6 my father / us home (take)
  _____

7 Steve / a place to sit and eat his cake (find)
  _____

8 we / a DVD (watch)
  _____

4 ★★☆ José Luis didn't have a good weekend. Complete the sentences with the simple past form of the verbs in the list.

~~be~~ | be | decide | do | not do | not rain
not work | rain | try | use | want

0 Last weekend _____*was*_____ terrible.

1 It _____ all day on Saturday.

2 I _____ anything interesting.

3 I _____ to watch a movie, but our Internet service _____ .

4 My brother _____ the computer for his homework all afternoon.

5 I _____ to go out, but it was too cold and wet.

6 But, it _____ on Sunday. Great!

7 So I _____ to ride my bike to the park.

8 But one of the tires on my bike _____ flat.

9 What _____ you _____ last weekend?

5 ★★★ Complete the text with the simple past form of the verbs in parentheses.

Sarah ^{0} ___went___ (go) to San Diego last weekend with three friends. They stayed in a student hotel. It was very cheap, but the rooms ^{1}_____ (not be) very nice. Sarah ^{2}_____ (share) a room with Lisa. The hotel has a café, and on Friday evening they ^{3}_____ (eat) dinner there because they were tired from the trip. But Jason and Alex ^{4}_____ (not like) the pizza very much.

On Saturday morning, Sarah and Lisa ^{5}_____ (go) to the Natural History Museum. They ^{6}_____ (see) a dodo and a mammoth. Jason and Alex ^{7}_____ (not want) to look at old animals, so they ^{8}_____ (spend) the morning in an art gallery instead. In the evening they ^{9}_____ (take) the bus downtown to the movies, but they ^{10}_____ (not watch) one because it was very expensive. So they ^{11}_____ (have) a pizza, and this time the boys were happy!

Simple past (questions) SB page 105

6 ★★★ Use the information in Exercise 5 and write questions for these answers.

0
A _Where did Sarah go last weekend?_
B She went to San Diego.

1
A Where _____
B In a hotel.

2
A What _____ on Friday?
B A pizza in the café.

3
A What _____
B A dodo and a mammoth.

4
A Where _____
B In the art gallery.

5
A What _____
B Pizza.

Pronunciation

Simple past: irregular verbs
Go to page 121.

🔊

---

could / couldn't SB page 107

7 ★★☆ Last year Brad broke his leg and they put it in a cast. What could he do? What couldn't he do? Use the phrases in the list.

do his homework | eat a pizza | go swimming listen to music | ~~play soccer~~ | play the guitar ride a bike | text his friends | ~~watch TV~~

0 _Brad could watch TV._
0 _He couldn't play soccer._
1 He _____
2 He _____
3 He _____
4 He _____
5 He _____
6 He _____
7 He _____

GET IT RIGHT! 👁
Simple past

We always use the base form of the verb after *didn't* (in negative sentences) or *Did* (in questions).
✓ I **didn't go** to the party last Saturday.
✗ I ~~didn't went~~ to the party last Saturday.
✓ **Did** you **visit** the Science Museum?
✗ ~~Did you visited~~ the Science Museum.

Correct the sentences.

0 He didn't finished his homework.
   He didn't finish his homework.

1 Jack didn't liked the party.

   _____

2 We didn't paid much for lunch at the zoo yesterday.

   _____

3 Did they enjoyed their holiday?

   _____

4 We didn't knew where it was, but finally we found it.

   _____

5 Bill's friend didn't ate any cake at the party.

   _____

6 Where did you went after the party?

VOCABULARY

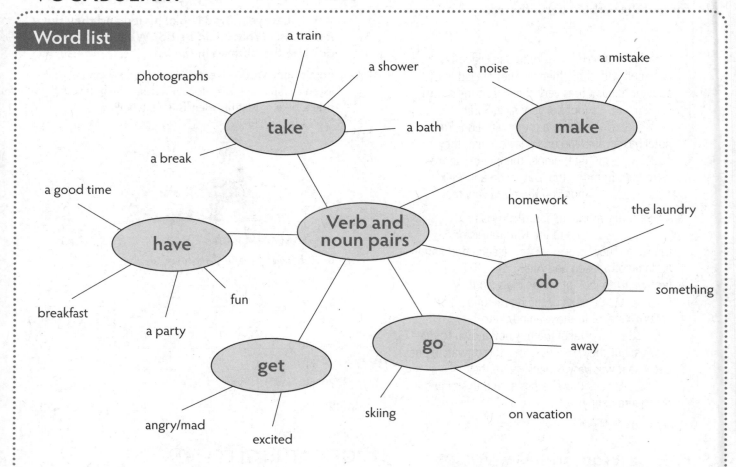

a train
a shower
photographs
take
a bath
a break
a noise
a mistake
make

a good time
have
Verb and noun pairs
homework
the laundry
do
something

breakfast
a party
fun
get
angry/mad
excited
go
away
skiing
on vacation

interesting
beautiful
clean
positive
smart
safe
nice

Adjectives

ugly
boring
dirty
negative
stupid
dangerous
terrible

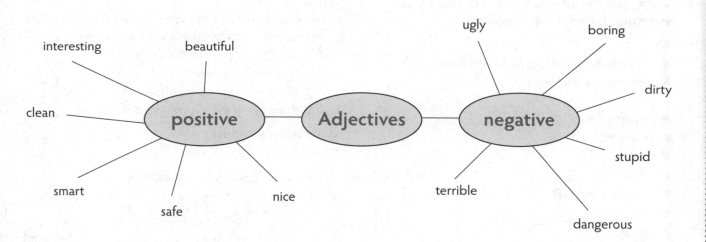

Key words in context

afraid	I'm **afraid** of spiders. I can't even look at one!
become	After we moved to California, my mom **became** a nurse.
extinct	There are no more dodos in the world. They are **extinct** now.
horn	Giraffes have little **horns** on their heads.
island	Australia and Madagascar are very big **islands**.
ride	You can **ride** my new bike if you want to.
scared	I was **scared** because the dog was big and angry!
teeth	Birds don't have **teeth**.
woods	It was very dark in the **woods** because there were a lot of trees.

Verb and noun pairs SB page 104

1 ★★☆ **Read the sentences. Are the underlined words correct (✓) or incorrect (✗)? Write the correct words.**

0 I always <u>do</u> my homework. ✓

0 I <u>do</u> breakfast every morning. ✗
   have

1 I'm tired. Let's <u>take</u> a break now. ☐

2 We just <u>went</u> the shopping for the party. ☐

3 Try not to <u>do</u> a lot of mistakes. ☐

4 I want to sleep. Please don't <u>have</u> a lot of noise. ☐

5 We <u>made</u> some great photos on vacation. ☐

6 Did you <u>do</u> a good time at the party? ☐

2 ★★☆ **Complete the sentences with the correct verb in the correct form.**

0 They ____*went*____ skiing last winter.

1 I always _____ excited the day before my birthday.

2 I always _____ something on the weekend. I never stay home.

3 We live near an airport. The planes _____ a lot of noise every day.

4 Our weekend was fantastic! We _____ a party at our house.

5 Every day, when I wake up, I _____ a bath.

6 We weren't hungry, so we didn't _____ breakfast.

7 Do you always _____ the bus to school?

Adjectives SB page 107

3 ★★☆ **Unscramble the letters to make adjectives. Then look at the pictures and write the phrases.**

0	1	2	3	4
enci	ercvel	tydri	putdis	regnoudas

5	6	7	8	9
bletirre	gluy	teulauibf	tersniginet	lance

0 *a nice gorilla*
1 _____
2 _____
3 _____
4 _____

5 _____
6 _____
7 _____
8 _____
9 _____

4 ★★☆ **Complete the puzzle. What's the mystery word?**

1 I don't like this movie, it's really _____ .

2 I don't like this food at all. It's _____ .

3 Bears can sometimes be _____ .

4 I don't like that house. I think it's _____ .

5 I have to wash my parents' car because it's very _____ .

6 The class today was great. It was really _____ .

7 Some big cities aren't very _____ at night.

8 Hey! That was a really _____ thing to do!

9 I must do the laundry. I don't have any _____ clothes.

Mystery word: _____

READING

1 REMEMBER AND CHECK (Circle) the correct answers (A, B, or C). Then look at the article on page 103 of the Student's Book and check your answers.

0 Erin took a group of _____ people for a ride in the woods.

   A three   **B** fifteen   **C** eight

1 Erin's horse, Tonk, was _____ .

   A white   **B** black   **C** brown

2 The grizzly bear was _____ .

   A asleep   **B** angry   **C** scared

3 The boy's horse _____ .

   A stopped   **B** ran away   **C** jumped over a fence

4 The boy _____ .

   A fell off his horse   **B** jumped to the ground   **C** kicked his horse

5 Erin and Tonk ran at the bear _____ .

   A once   **B** twice   **C** three times

2 Read the stories. What are the dogs' names? _____ _____

HERO DOGS

Story 1

Nick Lamb is 13 years old and he's deaf (he can't hear). He lives in Indiana in the U.S. He has a dog named Ace. One day, Nick was home alone. His parents were at work. After lunch, Nick fell asleep in his room. Ace smelled fire in the house. He went into Nick's room, but Nick couldn't hear him, so he jumped on him to wake him up. Nick jumped up, covered his nose and mouth with his T-shirt, and ran out of the house with Ace. Then he called 911 – the emergency number in the U.S. – and his mother. When the firefighters arrived, they could see the fire in the garage. No one was hurt.

Story 2

Roger Wilday is 68 years old and lives in Birmingham, England. One day, he went for a walk in a small park with his dog, Jade. Suddenly, Jade ran off into the woods. She didn't come back when Mr. Wilday called her, so he went to find her. When he saw her, Jade was standing beside a plastic bag. Mr. Wilday tried to move Jade, but he couldn't. Suddenly, Mr. Wilday saw a small arm and heard crying. There was a little baby in the bag! Mr. Wilday called the police, who quickly took the baby to the hospital. The nurse at the hospital said the baby was only about 24 hours old. The doctor said that the baby was lucky that the dog found her. The doctors named the baby "Jade," and she's fine now.

3 Read the sentences and <u>underline</u> the incorrect information. Then write correct sentences.

Story 1

0 <u>Nick's mother</u> was home alone.   *Nick was home alone.*

1 Nick was in the yard.   _____

2 Nick covered his eyes and mouth.   _____

3 The fire was in the backyard.   _____

Story 2

4 Mr. Wilday went for a walk downtown with his dog.   _____

5 The dog ran into the water.   _____

6 Mr. Wilday took the baby to the hospital.   _____

7 The baby was about one week old.   _____

DEVELOPING WRITING

The life of an animal

1 Read the text. Which animal wrote it? Check (✓) the correct animal.

Why we died out

We were great animals. We were very happy for a long time. We lived in a place that was a long way from the ocean. It wasn't very warm, but that was OK. We could stay warm in the cold weather because we had thick coats.

But we had a serious problem. Other animals – we called them "people" – wanted to kill us and eat us. Well, we didn't like that very much, of course. But we watched out for the people, and we lived.

And then, a long time ago, the weather changed. The days got hot. Our thick coats became a problem, and we couldn't live. Then, we died out.

dodo ☐

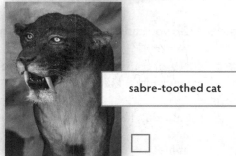

sabre-toothed cat ☐

woolly rhinoceros ☐

2 Complete the sentences with *but* or *because*.

1 We were happy, _____ there was a problem.

2 We weren't cold _____ we had thick coats.

3 It was cold, _____ that was OK for us.

4 People killed us _____ they wanted to eat us.

5 We lived in a cold place, _____ the weather started to change.

6 We died out _____ we couldn't live in the hot weather.

3 Look at the text in Exercise 1 and match the adjectives with the nouns.

1 thick ☐   a weather

2 cold ☐   b problem

3 great ☐   c coat

4 serious ☐   d animals

4 Choose one of the other two animals in the pictures. Look at the text on page 106 of the Student's Book and make notes about the animal in your notebook. Think about these questions.

● Where and when did it live?

● What was special about it?

● What could/couldn't it do?

● Why did it die out?

5 Use your notes in Exercise 4 and write a short text about the animal.

Why we died out

We were _____

_____

We lived _____

_____

We had _____

_____

We could/couldn't _____

_____

Then, _____

_____

We died out because _____

_____

LISTENING

1 🔊46 **Listen to Tommy and his grandfather. What did Grandpa have when he was young?**

cards ☐

computers ☐

envelopes ☐

Internet ☐

letters ☐

cell phones ☐

paper ☐

pens ☐

2 🔊46 **Listen again. Mark the sentences T (true) or F (false).**

0	Tommy went in a time machine.	F
1	The professor made a time machine.	☐
2	The time machine only went back ten years.	☐
3	The kids saw a dodo.	☐
4	Grandpa had a computer 50 years ago.	☐
5	He had a phone.	☐
6	He could walk around with his phone.	☐
7	Grandpa didn't use a computer to do his homework.	☐
8	Tommy thinks life was easier then.	☐

DIALOGUE

1 **Complete the dialogue with the words and phrases in the list.**

after that | and | because | ~~but~~
You poor thing | Then

BELLA Did you have a good weekend?

KEN Yes, it was great. I went to Miguel's party.

BELLA Oh, right. He invited me too, ⁰ _but_ I couldn't go.

KEN Why not?

BELLA My aunt and uncle were here for the weekend, ¹_____ they wanted to take us out.

KEN That's nice. Where did you go?

BELLA We went to the theater. It was really boring.

KEN ²_____ !

BELLA But ³_____ we went out for pizza. That was good! ⁴_____ I ordered a big dessert. I couldn't eat it all, I was so full.

KEN That's like me at the party. I couldn't dance ⁵_____ I was really tired from soccer on Saturday!

2 **Read the dialogue again and answer the questions.**

1 Why couldn't Bella go to the party?

_____

2 Why couldn't Bella eat all her dessert?

_____

3 Why couldn't Ken dance at the party?

_____

PHRASES FOR FLUENCY

SB page 109

1 **Unscramble the letters to make expressions.**

0 dunylsed _suddenly_

1 lal thrig. _____

2 uoy orpo hgtni! _____

3 thwa phedapen? _____

2 **Complete the dialogue with the expressions in Exercise 1.**

ANNIE Do you know what happened to me last weekend?

KATE No, of course not. I wasn't with you last weekend. ⁰ _What happened?_

ANNIE ¹_____ , I'll tell you. On Saturday, I was in the café on Main Street, and ²_____ someone waved at me!

KATE So? Who was it?

ANNIE It was Jennifer Hall.

KATE Jenny Hall? Are you sure? Jenny's in Canada! She went last year.

ANNIE Well, she's here on vacation. But it was terrible.

KATE Why?

ANNIE I couldn't remember her name! I called her Jessica, and she got really angry with me! She yelled at me!

KATE Oh, ³_____ I'm sure that was terrible for you!

Sum it up

TIME-O-TRON TRAVEL

See the dinosaurs!

Talk to William Shakespeare!

Watch the Egyptians building the pyramids!

Welcome to the wonderful world of Time-O-Tron Travel.

As you know, last year the famous Professor Godbole of Delhi University invented the

Time-O-Tron Travel Machine

Now, you can go into the past! (Sorry, no future travel yet – maybe next year!)

Sit in the **Time-O-Tron**, choose your time in the past – and whoosh! Away you go!

We are offering one-day trips into the past for only $1,000,000! That's right! Only a million dollars for 24 hours in any past time that you choose.

But here's some really good news – we have a contest and the five lucky winners will get a free one-day trip in the **Time-O-Tron**!

To enter the contest:

*   write us to say what time in the past you'd like to visit and why (write no more than 25 words)
*   start your entry with "I want to go to …"

Here are two examples to help you.

"I want to go to pre-history and see the dinosaurs because they're fantastic animals!" (Monika, Germany)

"I want to go to 1998 because that's when my country won the World Cup, but I wasn't alive then!" (Pierre, France)

But remember – if you win, you must go to the time you wrote about!

GOOD LUCK!

Send your ideas to us at: Time-O-Tron Travel, P.O. Box 2020, London

---

1 Read the ad. Mark the sentences T (true) or F (false).

1 A man in New York invented the travel machine. ☐

2 You can travel to the past and into the future. ☐

3 You can buy a trip into the past for a million dollars. ☐

4 The time trips are for one day. ☐

5 Five people can win the contest. ☐

6 If you win, you can go to any past time that you want. ☐

2 Imagine there's a time machine! Where would you like to go? Write an entry for the contest in your notebook. Follow the instructions in the ad.

*   Say what time in the past you want to travel to, and why.
*   Write a paragraph, beginning with "I want to go to …"

GRAMMAR
Comparative adjectives
`SB page 112`

1 ★☆☆ <u>Underline</u> the comparative adjective in each sentence.

0   A train is <u>quicker</u> than a car.

1   His computer is more expensive than my computer.

2   Surfing is more dangerous than ice skating.

3   The weather in winter is worse than in summer.

4   Spanish is easier than English.

5   Your photo is better than my photo.

6   My house is farther from school than your house.

7   Salad is healthier than hot dogs.

8   Their house is bigger than our house.

2 ★☆☆ Complete the table with the correct adjective forms.

Adjective	Comparative
0 dirty	*dirtier*
1 beautiful	
2 cold	
3	curlier
4 hot	
5	cleaner
6	shorter
7 ugly	
8	more boring
9 sad	
10 warm	
11 lovely	
12	slower
13	more interesting

3 ★★☆ Look at the table and mark the sentences T (true) or F (false). Correct the false sentences.

	Leaves Washington, D.C.	Arrives New York	Price
train	10:00 a.m.	1:00 p.m.	$123
bus	9:00 a.m.	1:20 p.m.	$28
plane	10:10 a.m.	11:30 a.m.	$254

0   The bus is cheaper than the train. `T`

1   The bus arrives later than the train. ☐

2   The bus is slower than the plane. ☐

3   The bus is more expensive than the plane. ☐

4   The plane is faster than the train. ☐

5   The plane arrives earlier than the train. ☐

4 ★★★ Use the table in Exercise 3 to write sentences. Use comparative adjectives.

0   bus / early / train
The bus leaves earlier than the train.

1   train / fast / bus

2   plane / expensive / bus

3   train / slow / plane

4   plane / late / bus

5   bus / cheap / train

Pronunciation
Word stress: comparatives
Go to page 121. 🔊

5 ★★★ Look at the pictures and write sentences to compare the two taxi companies. Use the adjectives in the list to help you.

big | ~~clean~~ | dangerous | dirty |
expensive | fast | good | safe

0 _Linda's Limos are cleaner than Tom's Taxis._
1 _____
2 _____
3 _____
4 _____
5 _____
6 _____
7 _____

6 ★★★ Complete the sentences so they are true for you.

1 I'm _____ than my parents.
2 My best friend is _____ than me.
3 English class is _____ than math class.
4 Dogs are _____ than cats.
5 Summer is _____ than winter.
6 Cars are _____ than trains.

one / ones `SB page 115`

7 ★☆☆ Circle the correct options.

0 Can I take a look at those shoes? The *one* / *ones* in the window.
1 Don't make a sandwich for me. I don't want *one* / *ones*.
2 I like most movies, but I don't like *one* / *ones* about war.
3 I can't give you a pen because I don't have *one* / *ones*.
4 I have some cookies. Would you like *one* / *ones*?
5 I'm interested in cars. I really like Italian *one* / *ones*.

8 ★★☆ Write *one* into the mini-dialogues.

0 A Where's your house?
   B My house is the first⌄on the left.
                        one
1 A How was your birthday?
   B Great. I got lots of gifts, but my favorite was a book from my dad.
2 A Which dress did you buy?
   B Well, I love blue, so I bought the blue.
3 A How is your new computer?
   B It's faster than my old and it's easier to use.
4 A Is your brother over there?
   B Yes, he's the with the glasses.

GET IT RIGHT! 👁

one and *ones*

We use *one* or *ones* after an adjective when we want to avoid repeating a noun.
✓ *I like this song, it's a good* **one**.
✗ *I like this song, it's a good song.*
✓ *I wore my new shoes – the red* **ones**.
✗ *I wore my new shoes – the red shoes.*

Replace one of the nouns with *one* or *ones*.

0 How much are the cookies? I like the peanut butter cookies.
   How much are the cookies? I like the peanut butter ones.

1 These tickets are expensive. We can find cheaper tickets.
   _____

2 This pen isn't good. I have a better pen in my bag.
   _____

3 The black jeans are too big. The blue jeans are much better.
   _____

4 All of the buses go there, but the green bus is the fastest.
   _____

5 Where are my black shoes? They were by my red shoes.
   _____

VOCABULARY

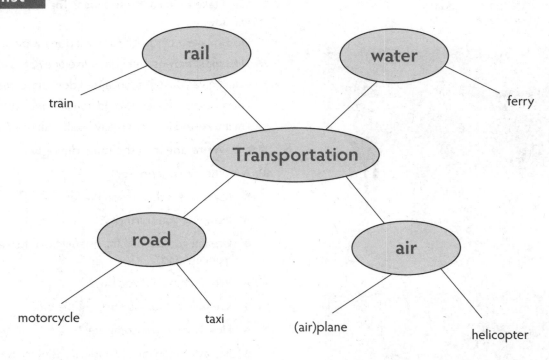

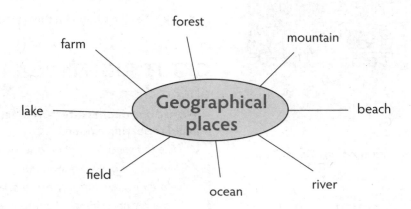

Key words in context

airport	The plane arrives at the **airport** at 10:00 p.m.
host	My mom's the **host** of a TV show. She talks to interesting people about old houses.
medal	The winner of the race gets a **medal**.
one-way	I'm not coming back from Toronto, so I only need to buy a **one-way** ticket.
platform	The Boston train leaves from **platform** 12.
pollute	Cars **pollute** the air.
round-trip	I want to go to Toronto and then come back again, so I need to buy a **round-trip** ticket.
side	The train station is over there on the other **side** of the bridge.
ticket	You need a **ticket** to travel on the bus.
traffic	There's a lot of **traffic** in our town. It's terrible for drivers.
trip	The **trip** from my house to school is about ten minutes by bike.

Transportation SB page 112

1 ★☆☆ Find and (circle) six types of transportation in the word snake.

gemotorcycleasehelicopternmbdplanerkutaxilfqferryipatrainbgh

2 ★★☆ Unscramble the column titles and complete the table with words from Exercise 1.

no het ardo ⁰*on the road*	no sairl ¹_____	ni eth ria ²_____	no tware ³_____
motorcycle			

3 ★★★ Match the words in Exercise 1 with the definitions.

0 It flies in the air, but it doesn't have wings.   *helicopter*

1 It travels on rails and is very long.   _____

2 It flies in the air. It has wings.   _____

3 It travels on water and carries a lot of people.   _____

4 You pay someone to drive you.   _____

5 It goes on the road, and it has only two wheels.   _____

Geographical places SB page 115

4 ★★☆ Find the places in the word search.

O	C	E	A	N	B	W	W	M
H	E	E	O	E	G	S	O	S
F	V	S	A	D	R	U	E	E
O	M	C	D	U	N	A	K	R
R	H	R	R	T	B	A	E	U
E	T	P	A	B	L	V	S	C
S	X	I	E	F	I	P	B	T
T	N	C	K	R	R	T	D	B
Z	D	L	E	I	F	L	O	V

5 ★★☆ Match the geographical places with the famous examples.

1 mountain ☐

2 lake ☐

3 river ☐

4 beach ☐

5 ocean ☐

a The Nile, The Amazon, The Rio Grande

b Aconcagua, K2, Kilimanjaro

c Copacabana, Bondi, Kuta

d Pacific, Atlantic, Indian

e Michigan, Titicaca, Victoria

6 ★★★ Complete the sentences with examples from your own country.

1 My favorite beach is _____.

2 The highest mountain is _____.

3 A famous lake is _____.

4 The longest river is _____.

5 _____ is a good place to go on vacation.

6 _____ is a beautiful place in the summer / winter.

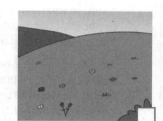

READING

1 REMEMBER AND CHECK **Mark the sentences T (true) or F (false). Then look at the article on page 111 of the Student's Book and check your answers.**

0	Walking is the best way to make a short trip in Manhattan.	T
1	The hosts made a trip from Battery Park to Central Park.	☐
2	One of the hosts walked.	☐
3	The boat was faster than public transportation.	☐
4	The hosts were unhappy the bike won.	☐
5	The hosts decided that the car won.	☐

2 **Read the blog. Which of these types of transportation is <u>not</u> mentioned?**

☐ ☐ ☐ ☐ ☐ ☐

Racing around the world!

My favorite book is called *Around the World in 80 Days*. It's the story of a man who makes a bet that he can travel around Earth in less than 80 days. Of course, these days that's not difficult, but the book is from more than 100 years ago.

I love the idea of adventure and exploration, so it's no surprise that my favorite TV show is called *The Amazing Race*. It's a really exciting show. Teams race against each other around the world to win a big prize. There are two people on each team, for example: a husband and wife, a father and son, or best friends. It's important that they have a good relationship because the race is really difficult and they need to be strong and help each other.

The race takes them all over the world, and they use a lot of different types of transportation. They use planes, of course, to make the longer trips, but they also use boats, taxis, buses, helicopters, bikes, cars, trains – any type of transportation that makes their trip quicker.

At the beginning of each show, the host gives the teams ideas about where they have to go. The last team to arrive at that place leaves the show. When there are only three teams left, they race to the final place. The team that arrives first usually wins a lot of money.

I love this show because you see a lot of really exciting places all over the world. One day I want to be on the show.

3 **Read the blog again and match the sentence halves.**

0	*Around the World in 80 Days*	g	a	between teams of two people.
1	*The Amazing Race*	☐	b	all over the world.
2	The race is	☐	c	leaves the show.
3	The people on the teams	☐	d	gets a lot of money.
4	The teams race	☐	e	is a TV show.
5	The teams use	☐	f	a lot of different types of transportation.
6	The last team to arrive	☐	g	is a famous book.
7	In the final show	☐	h	know each other.
8	The winning team	☐	i	there are only three teams.

4 **Do you want to be on *The Amazing Race*? Why or why not? Write a short paragraph (35–50 words).**

DEVELOPING WRITING

Writing about a trip

1 Read about Eduardo and Daniela's favorite trip and complete the table.

	from	to	transportation	time it takes	why I like it
Eduardo					
Daniela					

Eduardo

My favorite trip is the one I do every Sunday morning to play soccer. I leave my house at about ten o'clock and get on my bike to ride the two kilometers to the park. It takes me about 15 minutes. At the park I meet my friends, and we play soccer for two hours. Then I get on my bike and ride back home. I like the trip there because I get excited about playing soccer. I don't like the trip back so much because I'm usually pretty tired. But when I have a good game, the trip back is great, too, because I think about the game.

Daniela

The trip I like most is the one from my house to the airport. My dad lives in Seattle, and three times every year I fly there to spend time with him. The day starts really early. The taxi picks me up from my house at 4:00 a.m.! But that's OK, because I'm always really happy. It's only 30 minutes to the airport, but I can't wait to get there. The flight to Seattle is about four hours. It's OK, but I'm usually a little nervous about flying. My dad always meets me at the airport and then he drives me to his house. We don't stop talking the whole way. I never like the trip back. I'm always really sad to leave.

2 Read the texts again and complete the sentences.

0 Eduardo likes the trip to the park because *he gets excited about playing soccer.*

1 He doesn't like the trip back because _____

2 Daniela likes going to the airport because _____

3 She doesn't like the trip home because _____

3 Make notes to complete the table so it is true for you.

	from	to	transportation	time	why I like it
Me					

4 Use your notes to write a text about your favorite trip. Write 35–50 words.

My favorite trip is _____

_____

_____

_____

_____

LISTENING

1 Listen to the dialogue. Where is Julia? Who is she talking to?

_____

2 Listen again and (circle) the correct answers (A, B, or C).

0 Where does Julia want to go?

  A Charleston

  (B) Savannah

  C Atlanta

1 What time is the next train?

2 How often is there a train?

  A every 15 minutes

  B every 30 minutes

  C every 50 minutes

3 How long is the trip?

  A 40 minutes

  B 35 minutes

  C 45 minutes

4 When is Julia returning?

  A today

  B tomorrow

  C on the weekend

5 How much is the ticket?

  A $7.80

  B $8.70

  C $17.80

6 What platform is the train leaving from?

  A 3

  B 4

  C 5

7 What time does Julia get the train?

A

B

C

DIALOGUE

(Circle) the correct options. Then put the dialogue in order.

☐	CLERK	The trip is three ¹_quarters_ / _halves_ of an hour.
☐	CLERK	OK, that's $5.50, please.
☐	CLERK	Platform 5. Have a ²_good_ / _boring_ trip.
☐	CLERK	Let me see. There's a train every 15 minutes, so the next one is at 1:20.
☐	CLERK	Do you want a one-way or a round-trip ticket?
1	CLERK	Good afternoon. ³_How_ / _Who_ can I help you?
☐	WOMAN	That's great. And how long does it take?
☐	WOMAN	Thank you.
☐	WOMAN	I want to ⁴_go_ / _come_ to New Haven. What time's the next train?
☐	WOMAN	Just one more thing. Which platform does the train leave ⁵_from_ / _at_?
☐	WOMAN	45 minutes. That's fast. Can I have a ticket, please?
☐	WOMAN	Round-trip, please. I'm coming back later today.

◾◾◾ TRAIN TO THiNK ◾◾◾

Comparing

1 Complete the diagram with the words in the list. Then use your own ideas and write six more words.

boring | dangerous | exciting | expensive | fun | relaxing

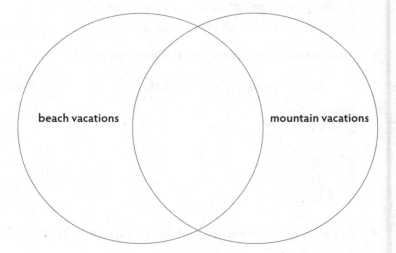

2 Write sentences to compare the two different types of vacations in Exercise 1.

_____

_____

_____

Answering open cloze questions

1 Read Danny's answers in the exam task below. How many did he get right? How many did he get wrong?

Complete the text about traveling to and from school. Write ONE word for each space.

I live **(0)** ......*in*...... a small town, and my school is about eight kilometers away. Most days I take the school bus. It stops outside my house **(1)** ......*at*...... 7:30 every morning. In the summer when the weather **(2)** .....*are*...... good, I usually ride my bike to school. It's quicker **(3)** ....*than*..... the bus because the bus stops all the time. The problem with the bike is when my school bag is too heavy. Then it **(4)** .....*isn't*.... fun!

Sometimes I wake up late and **(5)** ......*mis*..... the school bus. Mom takes me to school **(6)** ......*in*...... the car. She doesn't like this **(7)** ..*because*.. she needs to get to work, too. Once I missed the bus home and I had to **(8)** ....*tired*....home. It took me more than **(9)** ..*half an*...hour to walk. I don't want **(10)** ......*to*......do that again.

Reading and writing tip

- Read the instructions carefully. Underline the key words. Words like *circle*, *check*, *choose*, and *underline* tell you how to complete the question. Look for other important information, for example, *Only write one word*.
- When you are finished, read your answers again. Did you follow the instructions? Did you use the correct type of word (verb, noun, adjective, etc.)? Did you use the singular and plural forms correctly? Is your spelling correct?
- Don't leave any blanks. If you don't know the answer, guess!

---

2 Put Danny's mistakes under the correct heading. Write the number.

Used more than one word	Used the wrong type of word (adjective instead of verb)	Used singular and plural forms incorrectly	Used incorrect spelling
9			

3 Correct Danny's mistakes. Write the correct words next to the numbers in Exercise 2.

4 Complete the text about favorite vacations. Write ONE word for each space.

My favorite vacations **(0)** .....**are**..... beach vacations. I like the sun **(1)** .... the sea. I usually go on beach vacations **(2)** .... the summer with my family. Sometimes Dad drives and sometimes we **(3)** .... the train. Last year we went **(4)** .... vacation in the countryside. We stayed on **(5)** .... farm. There was a river and a lake and a lot **(6)** .... fields, too. It was OK, but I prefer beach vacations. The weather by the ocean is usually hotter **(7)** .... in the countryside. Dad wants to **(8)** .... on vacation in the mountains this year. I'm **(9)** .... happy about that idea. I don't want another year away **(10)** .... the beach.

CONSOLIDATION

LISTENING

1 ◀))49 **Listen to Andrew and** (circle) **the correct answers (A, B, or C).**

1 How old is Andrew's brother?
  A eight   B nine   C ten
2 At the zoo, which animals scared Andrew's brother?
  A the elephants B the lions   C the tigers
3 How many jaguars were there?
  A two   B three   C four

2 ◀))49 **Listen again and answer the questions.**

1 Why did Andrew's family go to the zoo?
  _____

2 Who took photos at the zoo?
  _____

3 What was Andrew happy about?
  _____

4 What did Andrew think about the visit to the zoo?
  _____

5 Why was Andrew sorry for the jaguars?
  _____

6 What two things does Andrew think zoo animals need?
  _____

GRAMMAR

3 **Complete the sentences with the correct form of the words in parentheses.**

1 Yesterday I _____ some money on the street. (find)

2 For my last birthday, my parents _____ me tickets to a concert. (give)

3 My friends and I _____ to the movies three times last weekend. (go)

4 I got home late last night, but I _____ any noise. (not make)

5 Yesterday's quiz was _____ than the one on Friday. (difficult)

6 _____ you _____ that movie on TV last Sunday night? (see)

7 My grades are _____ than my brother's. (bad)

8 I practice a lot and I'm getting _____ every day! (good)

9 I _____ many gifts for my birthday. (not get)

10 Are tigers _____ than jaguars? (big)

VOCABULARY

4 (Circle) **the odd one out in each list. Explain your reasons.**

0 safe   clean   (homework)
  a noun – the other two are adjectives

1 motorcycle   plane   helicopter
  _____

2 laundry   homework   a mistake
  _____

3 forest   ocean   lake
  _____

4 train   river   subway
  _____

5 a break   a good time   photos
  _____

6 boat   ferry   taxi
  _____

7 a mistake   a shower   a noise
  _____

8 breakfast   elephant   horse
  _____

9 field   beach   farm
  _____

5 **Use a word or phrase from Exercise 4 to complete each sentence.**

1 Shh! Don't make _____ or that pretty bird will fly away.

2 We went for a walk in the _____ this morning. The trees were very beautiful.

3 My mom doesn't like me riding my bike in the city. She thinks it isn't _____ .

4 This party's great. I'm really having _____ . Aren't you?

5 Her name's Kelly, but I made _____ and called her Karen.

6 I take _____ after soccer practice to get clean again!

7 We went to the beach, but I didn't swim in the _____ . I think it's dangerous.

8 I'm very tired. Let's take _____ and get some water.

DIALOGUE

6 Complete the dialogue with the words and phrases in the list. There are two extra ones.

All right | better | came | cheaper | could | couldn't | did
made | nice | suddenly | What happened | You poor thing

MIKE   How was your week at the beach?

MARIA   Oh, terrible. Everything went wrong.

MIKE   Oh, no. ¹_____ ?

MARIA   Well, first, we missed the train.

MIKE   But you finally got there?

MARIA   Oh, yes, we got there. We always stay at the same hotel. But it's very expensive,
        so this year Dad said, "Let's stay at a ²_____ hotel." I said, "If our usual hotel
        is more expensive, that's because it's ³_____ than the cheaper ones."
        But ⁴_____ he listen? No, he didn't. The hotel was terrible! I ⁵_____
        sleep at all. There were cars outside all night. They ⁶_____ a lot of noise!

MIKE   ⁷_____ . But what about the beach?

MARIA   The beach there is really ⁸_____ . We like it a lot. We went there on the first
        day – but ⁹_____ , it started to rain! We ¹⁰_____ home a day early.
        The vacation was … well, it was terrible.

READING

The Finger Lakes – there's nowhere more beautiful!

Are you thinking about taking a break? Then think about going to the Finger Lakes. This part of the U.S. has parks, forests, rivers – and, of course, lakes! No lake in the world is more beautiful than Lake Seneca or Lake Cayuga.

Some lakes have boat trips – spend an hour or two in the sun as you travel slowly along the lake.

There are small market towns like Penn Yan and Seneca Falls. Some of the stores there are more interesting than the ones you see in the big towns and cities. They're different and also much nicer. These small towns are safe, clean, and a lot of fun to visit.

The Finger Lakes area has many hotels and B&Bs/small bed-and-breakfast places. B&Bs are cheaper and often nicer than hotels, and even more comfortable!

It's easy to get to the Finger Lakes. Airplanes fly from Detroit, Chicago, and Philadelphia. From New York City it's even quicker: it's only a short road trip from there.

So, come and visit the Finger Lakes. We're looking forward to seeing you here!

7 Read the web page. Mark the sentences T (true) or F (false).

1   There are forests in the Finger Lakes area. ☐

2   Lake Seneca and Lake Cayuga aren't part of the Finger Lakes. ☐

3   It's possible to travel by boat on some of the lakes. ☐

4   Penn Yan is a big city. ☐

5   There aren't any stores in the Finger Lakes area. ☐

6   The small towns in the Finger Lakes are a little dirty. ☐

7   Hotels there are more expensive than B&Bs. ☐

WRITING

8 Write a paragraph about a nice area that you know. Use the questions to help you. Write 35–50 words.

● What is it called?

● What's good about it?

● What can people do there?

● How can you get there?

PRONUNCIATION

UNIT 7
The /ɔ/ vowel sound

1 🔊29 **Listen to these words. They all contain the /ɔ/ sound. Underline the sound in each word.**

   0 A<u>u</u>gust

   0 d<u>au</u>ghter

   1 tall

   2 awful

   3 draw

   4 call

   5 autumn

   6 fall

   7 ball

   8 walk

   9 water

2 **Complete the sentences with the words in Exercise 1.**

   0 In England, people call "fall" _autumn_ .

   1 It's a beautiful day. Let's go for a _____ .

   2 In _____ the leaves change to orange and it gets colder.

   3 Let's play soccer. Here's the _____ .

   4 My birthday's on the fourth of _____ .

   5 The tall girl with the curly hair is my _____ .

   6 This soup has too much salt. It's _____!

   7 In my free time, I like to _____ pictures.

   8 I'm thirsty. Can I have a glass of _____ , please?

   9 I am short, but my best friend is _____ .

   10 I need my phone to _____ my Dad.

3 🔊30 **Listen, check, and repeat.**

UNIT 8
Intonation: listing items

1 **Complete the lists. Then draw a ↑ and a ↓ to show where intonation rises and falls in each list.**

   arm | baseball | Brazil | catch | coat | headphones
   library | Russian | ~~June~~ | spring | stove | wife

       ↑   ↑   ↑   ↓

   0 March, April, May, and ___*June*___

   1 son, daughter, husband, and _____

   2 Japanese, British, _____ , and Turkish

   3 _____ , skirt, socks, and pants

   4 snowboarding, gymnastics, golf, and _____

   5 summer, _____ , winter, and fall

   6 watch, choose, throw, and _____

   7 _____ , shower, fridge, and chair

   8 Australia, Scotland, _____ , and Japan

   9 body, _____ , leg, and face

   10 tablet, GPS, _____ , and laptop

   11 _____ , restaurant, museum, and bank

2 🔊32 **Listen, check, and repeat.**

UNIT 9
Intonation: giving two choices

1   **▶36 Complete the dialogue with the words in the list. Then listen and check.**

chicken | fish | fries | ice cream
pineapple | ~~soup~~ | tea | water

⬆   ⬇

WAITER   Would you like ⁰___soup___ or salad?
WOMAN   Salad, please.

☐   ☐

WAITER   Chicken or ¹_____?
WOMAN   I think I'll have ²_____ today –
          with ³_____, please.
WAITER   Would you like dessert?
WOMAN   Yes, please.

☐   ☐

WAITER   Cake or ⁴_____?
WOMAN   I'd prefer fruit – some ⁵_____,
          please.
WAITER   Would you like something to drink?
WOMAN   Yes, please – just some ⁶_____.
          And a cup of ⁷_____ after the
          meal. Thank you.

2   **▶36 Draw ↑ or ↓ above the waiter's questions. Then listen, check, and repeat.**

UNIT 10
Simple past: regular verbs

1   **Say the verbs in the list in the past tense and decide if they are one syllable or two. Then write the verbs in the correct column.**

~~dance~~ | ~~hate~~ | help | like | live | need
play | start | wait | walk | want | work

One syllable	Two syllables
danced	hated

2   **▶38 Listen, check, and repeat.**

3   **▶39 Listen and complete the rule.**

We only say /ɪd/ when the last sound in the word is a
/ _____ / or a / _____ /.

UNIT 11
Simple past: irregular verbs

1   **Match the irregular verbs with the words that rhyme.**

A

0	found	e	a	thank
1	drank	☐	b	name
2	came	☐	c	you
3	knew	☐	d	caught
4	saw	☐	e	sound
5	thought	☐	f	wait
6	ate	☐	g	draw

B

7	took	☐	h	save
8	said	☐	i	boat
9	could	☐	j	bed
10	gave	☐	k	bad
11	wrote	☐	l	played
12	made	☐	m	good
13	had	☐	n	book

2   **▶45 Listen, check, and repeat.**

UNIT 12
Word stress: comparatives

1   **Write the comparative form of the adjectives. <u>Underline</u> the stressed syllable.**

0	slow	slower	8	big	_____
1	small	_____	9	hot	_____
2	quick	_____	10	funny	_____
3	cheap	_____	11	easy	_____
4	fast	_____	12	healthy	_____
5	cold	_____	13	happy	_____
6	safe	_____	14	far	_____
7	close	_____	15	good	_____

2   **▶47 Listen, check, and repeat.**

3   **Complete the rule.**

When adding -er to make a comparative, the ¹first /
second syllable is always stressed.

GRAMMAR REFERENCE

UNIT 7
can / can't for ability

1   We use *can/can't* to talk about ability.

*I **can** swim.*
*I **can't** drive a car.*
*He **can** play the guitar.*
*He **can't** sing.*

2   The form is *can/can't* + the base form of the verb. To make questions we use *Can* + subject + the base form of the verb. (We don't use *do/does* with *can* in questions or negative forms.)

*It's very small – I **can't read** it. (NOT: I don't can read …)*
***Can you play** this game? (NOT: Do you can play …?)*

3   Short answers are *Yes, … can* or *No, … can't.*

*Can he swim? **Yes, he can.***
*Can you sing? **No, I can't.***

Prepositions of time

We use different prepositions to talk about time.

1   With times of the day, we use *at.*

*School starts **at** eight o'clock.*
*The train leaves **at** seven thirty.*

2   With months and seasons, we use *in.*

*It always rains **in** December.*
*We play soccer **in** the winter.*

3   With days of the week, we use *on.*

*I always go to the movies **on** Saturday night.*
*There's a quiz in school **on** Monday.*

UNIT 8
Present continuous

1   We use the present continuous to talk about things that are happening at the moment of speaking.

*Please be quiet – I**'m watching** a movie.*
*They're in the dining room – they**'re eating** dinner.*
*Dad's in his office, but he **isn't working**.*
*Hey, Alex, **are** you **listening** to me?*

2   We form the present continuous with the simple present of *be* + the *-ing* form of the main verb. Questions and negatives are formed with the question/negative form of *be* + the *-ing* form of the main verb.

*I**'m watching** a movie, but I**'m not enjoying** it.*
*They**'re playing** soccer, but they a**ren't playing** well.*
***Are** you **having** a good time? Yes, we **are**.*
***Is** she **doing** her homework? No, she **isn't**.*

3   If the verb ends in -e, we omit the e before adding *-ing*. If the verb ends in a consonant + vowel + consonant, we double the consonant before adding *-ing*.

leave	*We're **leaving** now.*
get	*It's **getting** dark. Let's go home.*

like / don't like + -ing

When we use the verbs (*don't*) *like, love, hate,* and another verb, we usually use the *-ing* form of the other verb.

*We **love living** here.*
*I **like dancing** at parties.*
*She **doesn't like listening** to classical music.*
*They **hate going** to the theater.*

UNIT 9

must / must not

We use *must / must not* to talk about rules.

1 We use *must* to say that it's necessary to do something.

*We **must leave** now to arrive on time.*
*You **must go** to the doctor. You're really sick.*

2 We use *must not* to say that it's necessary NOT to do something.
*You **must not tell** anyone!*
*We **must not be** late.*

3 The form is *must / must not* + the base form of the verb. We don't use *do/does* in negative sentences.

*You must **ask** me first.*
*I must not **miss** my plane. (NOT: ~~I don't must miss my plane.~~)*

can (asking for permission)

1 We often use *Can I* + verb to ask for permission (to ask if it's OK) to do something.

*Can I **ask** a question, please?*
*Can I **watch** the game on TV now?*

2 We use *can* or *can't* to give or refuse permission.

*Can I **use** your book?*   *Yes, you **can**.*
                   *No, sorry, you **can't**. I'm using it.*

I'd like … / Would you like …?

1 We use *would ('d)* + *like* to ask for something, or to offer something, in a polite way. It is more polite than *want*.

*I'd **like** a sandwich, please.*
*Would you **like** some dessert?*

2 *I'd like* is the short form of *I would like*. We almost always use it in speaking and informal writing.

UNIT 10

Simple past: *be* (affirmative and negative)

1 We use the simple past form of *be* to talk about actions and events in the past.

*It **was** a beautiful day yesterday.*
*They **were** in school last Friday.*

2 We form the simple past of *be* like this:

Singular	Plural
I **was**	we **were**
you **were**	you **were**
he/she/it **was**	they **were**

3 We form the negative by adding *not* (*was not*, *were not*). In speaking and informal writing we almost always use the short forms *wasn't* and *weren't*.

*I **wasn't** at home last night.*
*She **wasn't** at the party.*
*You **weren't** very happy yesterday.*
*They **weren't** with us at the concert.*

4 The simple past of *There is(n't) / There are(n't)* is *There was(n't) / There were(n't)*.

*There **was** a lot of rain yesterday.*
*There **weren't** any interesting shows on TV last night.*

Simple past: *be* (questions)

We form questions by putting the verb before the subject.

***Were** you late on Monday morning?*
***Was** she at the movies with you?*

Simple past: regular verbs

1 We use the simple past to talk about actions and events in the past.

*I **played** video games yesterday.*
*They **liked** the film on Friday.*

2 With regular verbs, we form the simple past by adding *-ed*. It is the same for all subjects.

*He **closed** the window.*
*The movie **ended** after midnight.*
*You **called** me three times last night.*
*We **wanted** to see them.*

3 When the verb ends in *-e*, we only add *-d*. When the verb ends in consonant + *-y*, we change the *y* to *i* and then we add *-ed*.

*We **loved** the concert on Sunday.*
*They **studied** for the test a long time.*

UNIT 11
Simple past: irregular verbs

1 Many English verbs are irregular. This means that the simple past forms are different – they don't have the usual *-ed* ending, for example:

go – went
make – made
give – gave
take – took
put – put

2 For every irregular verb, you need to remember the simple past form. There is a list of irregular verbs on page 128.

Simple past (negative)

We form negatives in the simple past with *didn't* (*did not*) and the base form of the verb. It's the same for both regular and irregular verbs. It's the same for all subjects.

talk	He talked, but I **didn't talk**.
like	I liked it, but you **didn't like** it.
give	They gave me a gift, but she **didn't give** me one.
go	He went to soccer practice, but he **didn't go** to school.
take	We took a trip to the beach, but we **didn't take** any photos.
make	They made things to sell, but they **didn't make** any money.

Simple past (questions)

1 We form questions in the simple past with *Did* + subject + the base form of the verb. It's the same for all verbs (regular and irregular) and for all subjects.

see	**Did** I **see** you downtown on Saturday? Yes, I saw you in the café!
do	**Did** you **do** the homework last night? I did it before class today.
go	**Did** your brother **go** to the same school? My brother went to a different school.
take	**Did** Grandma **take** you to the theater? She took me to the zoo.

could / couldn't

To talk about ability in the past, we use *could/couldn't* + the base form of a verb.

*When I was younger, I **could walk** on my hands.*
*We went to New York, but we **couldn't go** on the Empire State Building because it was closed.*

UNIT 12
Comparative adjectives

1 We use the comparative form of the adjective + *than* to compare two things.

*My sister is **younger than** me.*
*Australia is **smaller than** Brazil.*
*My new smartphone is **better than** my old phone.*

2 With short adjectives, we normally add *-er*.

*new – new**er***
*quiet – quiet**er***

With adjectives that end in *-e*, we just add *-r*.

*nice – nice**r***
*fine – fine**r***

With adjectives of two syllables that end with consonant + *-y*, we change the *y* to *i* and add *-er*.

*easy – eas**ier***
*healthy – health**ier***

With adjectives that end in consonant + vowel + consonant, we double the final consonant and add *-er*.

*big – bi**gger***
*hot – ho**tter***

3 With longer adjectives (adjectives with two or more syllables), we don't change the adjective – we put *more* in front of it.

*expensive – **more expensive***
*dangerous – **more dangerous***

4 Some adjectives are irregular. This means they have a different comparative form.

*good – **better***
*bad – **worse***
*far – **farther***

one / ones

1 Sometimes we don't want to repeat a noun. We can use *one* or *ones* instead of repeating it.

*These cookies are delicious – I want another (~~cookie~~) **one**.*
*These shoes are very expensive – I want cheaper (~~shoes~~) **ones**.*

2 We use *one* to replace a singular noun, and *ones* to replace a plural noun.

*This red shirt is OK, but the blue **one** is nicer.* (**one** replaces **shirt**)
*I don't want to play these old games. Let's buy some new **ones**.* (**ones** replaces **games**)

IRREGULAR VERBS

Base form	Simple past
be	was
begin	began
buy	bought
can	could
catch	caught
choose	chose
come	came
do	did
draw	drew
drink	drank
drive	drove
eat	ate
fall	fell
feel	felt
find	found
fly	flew
get	got
give	gave
go	went
have	had
hear	heard
keep	kept
know	knew
leave	left
light	lit

Base form	Simple past
make	made
meet	met
pay	paid
put	put
read /riːd/	read /red/
ride	rode
run	ran
say	said
see	saw
sell	sold
send	sent
sing	sang
sit	sat
sleep	slept
speak	spoke
stand	stood
take	took
teach	taught
tell	told
think	thought
understand	understood
wake	woke
wear	wore
write	wrote

Acknowledgments

The authors and publishers acknowledge the following sources of copyright material and are grateful for the permissions granted. While every effort has been made, it has not always been possible to identify the sources of all the material used or to trace all copyright holders. If any omissions are brought to our notice, we will be happy to include the appropriate acknowledgments on reprinting.

Corpus

Development of this publication has made use of the Cambridge English Corpus (CEC). The CEC is a computer database of contemporary spoken and written English, which currently stands at over one billion words. It includes British English, American English, and other varieties of English. It also includes the Cambridge Learner Corpus, developed in collaboration with Cambridge English Language Assessment. Cambridge University Press has built up the CEC to provide evidence about language use that helps to produce better language teaching materials.

English Profile

This product is informed by the English Vocabulary Profile, built as part of English Profile, a collaborative program designed to enhance the learning, teaching, and assessment of English worldwide. Its main funding partners are Cambridge University Press and Cambridge English Language Assessment and its aim is to create a "profile" for English linked to the Common European Framework of Reference for Languages (CEF). English Profile outcomes, such as the English Vocabulary Profile, will provide detailed information about the language that learners can be expected to demonstrate at each CEF level, offering a clear benchmark for learners' proficiency. For more information, please visit www.englishprofile.org

Cambridge Dictionaries

Cambridge dictionaries are the world's most widely used dictionaries for learners of English. The dictionaries are available in print and online at dictionary.cambridge.org. Copyright © Cambridge University Press, reproduced with permission.

The publishers are grateful to the following for permission to reproduce copyright photographs and material:

T = Top, B = Below, L = Left, R = Right, C = Center, B/G = Background

p. 66 (TL): © RTimages / Alamy; p. 67 (CL): © Michael Burrell / Alamy; p. 68 (CR): © Action Plus Sports Images / Alamy; p. 68 (CR): © Bob Daemmrich / Alamy; p.

69 (TR): Veronika Surovtseva / Shutterstock; p. 69 (TR): Ken Reid / Getty Images; p. 70 (BL): © RTimages / Alamy; p. 76 (TR): Hero Images / Getty Images; p. 77 (BL): lkoimages / Shutterstock; p. 85 (CL): © Finnbarr Webster / Alamy; p. 85 (CL): © Edd Westmacott / Alamy; p. 85 (CL): © Elena Butinova / Alamy; p. 85 (CL): © HERA FOOD / Alamy; p. 85 (CL): © Keith Leighton / Alamy; p. 85 (CL): © Indigo Photo Agency / Alamy; p. 85 (CL): © Keith Leighton / Alamy; p. 85 (CL): © LAMB / Alamy; p. 85 (CL): © D. Hurst / Alamy; p. 85 (CL): © Nikreates / Alamy; p. 85 (CL): © Miles Davies / Alamy; p. 86 (TR): Pamela Moore / Getty Images; p. 86 (TR): Tetra Images / Getty Images; p. 86 (TR): valmas / Getty Images; p. 86 (TR): Karly Pope / Getty Images; p. 86 (TR): raphotography/ Getty Images; p. 86 (CR): © imageBROKER / Alamy; p. 88 (BL): Jacobs Stock Photography / Getty Images; p. 90 (BL): © Mike Blenkinsop / Alamy; p. 91 (TR): © GL Archive / Alamy; p. 95 (TL): © AF archive / Alamy; p. 95 (TR): © AF archive / Alamy; p. 96 (TL): © Pictorial Press Ltd / Alamy; p. 97 (CL): © The Art Archive / Alamy Stock Photo; p. 97 (CR): © Chris Hellier / Alamy; p. 99 (BR): Andersen Ross / Getty Images; p. 101 (TR): Izabela Habur / Getty Images; p. 104 (CR):The Indianapolis Fire Department; p. 104 (CR): BPM Media; p. 105 (BL): © Stocktrek Images, Inc / Alamy; p. 105 (BL): © Arterra Picture Library / Alamy; p. 105 (BL): © Stocktrek Images, Inc. / Alamy; p. 106 (CR): © PhotoAlto sas / Alamy; p. 107 (Top): Science Photo Library - MARK GARLICK/ Getty Images; p. 107 (Top): Denis Kozlenko / Getty Images; p. 107 (Top): Raul_Wong / Getty Images; p. 112 (CR): © Cultura Creative (RF) / Alamy; p. 112 (CR): Grant Faint / Getty Images; p. 114 (TL): kyoshino / Getty Images; p. 117 (DR): © Andre Jenny / Alamy Stock Photo.

Cover photographs by: (L): ©Tim Gainey/Alamy Stock Photo; (R): ©Yuliya Koldovska/Shutterstock.

The publishers are grateful to the following illustrators:

Christos Skaltsas (hyphen) 64, 65, 67, 70, 71, 75, 84, 94, 103, 109, 111 and Zaharias Papadopoulos (hyphen) 92, 112

The publishers are grateful to the following contributors:

hyphen: editorial, design, and project management; CityVox, LLC: audio recordings; Karen Elliott: Pronunciation sections; Matt Norton: Get it right! exercises